D0601180

The Ultimate Volunteer Guidebook for Young People

26 in 26
Neighborhood Resource Centers
26 Neighborhood Strategies in a 26 month time frame
A Grant Funded by the LSTA
(Library Services & Technology Act)

CITY OF
RIVERSIDE

Riverside Public Library

The *Ultimate Volunteer Guidebook for Young People*

Christine Reyna Maxwell, M. HR.

Foreword by Greg Baldwin, President of VolunteerMatch.org

WESTHOLME
Yardley

Copyright © 2008 Christine Reyna Maxwell

All rights reserved under International and Pan-American Copyright Conventions. No part of this book may be reproduced in any form or by any electronic or mechanical means, including information storage and retrieval systems, without permission in writing from the publisher, except by a reviewer who may quote brief passages in a review.

Westholme Publishing, LLC

Eight Harvey Avenue

Yardley, Pennsylvania 19067

Visit our Web site at www.westholmepublishing.com

First Printing: November 2007

10 9 8 7 6 5 4 3 2 1

ISBN: 978-1-59416-058-5

(ISBN 10: 1-59416-058-9)

Printed in United States of America

To my husband, Marc, I love you.
To my daughter, Meredith, I hope you grow up to have
a generous heart.

Contents

Foreword

Greg Baldwin, VolunteerMatch.org

It's not every day you get to do something good.

But every time you volunteer, you do something that helps not only others but also helps you feel better about yourself.

And it appears that youth may have a much better grasp of this concept than adults: In America, more than 15 million youth volunteer each year—an astounding 55%! That's nearly double the rate for adults, which equates to a lot of kids doing good.

This is particularly encouraging news, and when combined with the fact that nearly 70% of all adult volunteers have been volunteering since they were kids, it also illustrates that most of the volunteers in the United States learned the importance of service above self while still in their formative years.

At VolunteerMatch, we like to think we know a little bit about giving back. Our nonprofit service was created to make it easier for anyone to find a rewarding way to get involved and make a positive difference. This means that no matter how old you are or what your interests may be—the environment, animals, sports, music—you can quickly find a way to volunteer for a good cause.

Christine Reyna Maxwell has created a resource to help you do just that. *The Ultimate Volunteer Guidebook for Young People* provides excellent instruction, key tips, and motivating inspiration for young people who are interested in finding a great way to do something positive.

The future well-being of our neighborhoods and our country depends on a new generation of youth who are inspired to give and to actively get involved. If history is any indication, there has never been a better time to feel more confident about the tremendous promise for civic engagement, social responsibility, and community health.

Many hands make light work.

Introduction

Why volunteer?

Volunteering could be one of the most educational, inspiring, and exciting things you do in your lifetime. Donating your time to a worthwhile cause offers substantial rewards that will enrich your life. The personal rewards of volunteering include learning, cultural awareness, spiritual development, priorities reassessment, career development, and friendship.

What this guide tells you and your family.

The Ultimate Volunteer Guidebook for Young People is for children and families alike. This book gives the reader step-by-step directions on how to make a difference through volunteering. This guide is divided in five sections with fifty sample activities for practicing volunteers. Each activity section displays how-to directions, sample letters, thank-you notes, and flyers to get the amateur volunteer started. Each activity will help guide you to become the next ultimate volunteer.

Why is it important for children to volunteer?

To teach children well is to bring out the best in them. Most of us have a clear idea of wanting the best for our children. We want to make sure that they have enough food, clothes, hugs, toys, and friends. We want to give them the best education we can afford. We want them to do well, marry well, and have healthy children. We want them to be happy and successful. What's best for them is making sure they are happy and well rounded individuals. As children volunteer, they learn to help others and learn new experiences. A child who volunteers learns compassion and kindness for others. Volunteering educates children about the world around them-different cultures and religions.

How can volunteering benefit children?

Children who volunteer learn to take on new humanitarian projects that build confidence and responsibility. Volunteering gives children the opportunity to learn useful skills such as time management and money management, as well as record keeping. Children learn new skills and discover talents they never knew they had. Volunteering introduces children to new people of different walks of life. This can help children learn the value of diversity and human relations. Children can also build friendships to last a lifetime.

The value of volunteering as a family.

Volunteering as a family will have short-term and long-term rewards. The short-term reward is the impact you and your children will have on improving people's lives. The long-term reward is volunteering as a family will bring you and your family closer together. Working together as a family helps children learn team building, trust, and unity. Children also learn decision making through their parents. This helps develop their leadership skills throughout their involvement with their volunteer work. Volunteering as a family can introduce the entire family to new experiences and new skills. With this, the entire family will have wonderful memories to last a lifetime.

Guiding your children.

Being a parent is the most complex and important activity on the planet. Parents are a child's first and most important educator, yet they receive little or no training in what to do or how to do it. To teach a child well is to bring out the best in that child. What a child becomes is a result of four things: nature, nurture, opportunity, and effort. Nature is the essential character of a person. It's what the child is born with. Each child has a distinctive personality. Nurturing is how you, the parent, will help guide and nurture your child's personality and attributions. It is how a child is educated, how his or her contributions are recognized, supported, and shaped. Opportunity is how a child acts on his or her qualities and gives that child the possibility to become who that child is. Last, effort is a child's responsibility to respond to his or her opportunities and to practice his or her self worth.

Consider the virtues that are learned by volunteering.

Parents guide children in many ways. One is by sharing their knowledge, wisdom, and skills. Allowing children to participate in meaningful activities and gently guiding them to develop and master their own skills takes time. Giving a child a role in volunteering for a cause is a precious and valuable use of parental time. Virtues can be woven through these experiences. "Bobby you showed a lot of determination today. You showed service and humility when you were collecting school supplies for Sharpe Elementary School." In giving children the freedom to explore their abilities, you honor their strength, their creativity, purposefulness, and excellence.

How to get the most out of volunteering.

Educate yourself. Learn as much as you can about nonprofit organizations and about the people you're helping. Keep a journal of what you're learning and how you feel about the cause. Take pictures of the people you work with and have them sign an autograph book so that you can remember them and the experience forever.

Volunteering safely.

Always have your parents or an adult chaperone you when you are volunteering. If a stranger comes up to you and asks you to go to his or her car with him or her because he or she has something to donate to your cause, "Do not go by yourself"! Let your parents speak to this person. You always need parent supervision. Also, always make sure that the organization you want to donate to, raise money for, or volunteer with is a legitimate organization. Ask for their credentials. Find out if they are a nonprofit organization. If you are not sure about something, you can always call your city's Better Business Bureau.

Consider what you have to offer.

Exercise your expertise. Use your talent(s) to the best of your ability in the area that is needed in your volunteer work.

What issues are important to you and your family?

Direct your time and commitment to the issues that are most important to you and your family. Write down why these issues are important and how your volunteerism will affect your life and the life of others.

Learning something new with volunteering.

Although you may want to concentrate on the issues that are important to you when you first start volunteering, be sure to keep an open mind to other causes that you may not have originally thought of or ever heard of. This is a great way to learn something new.

Don't overcommit your schedule.

Take on one volunteer task at a time. Commit yourself to it wholeheartedly. Many times, people volunteer so much that they overschedule themselves. They are torn and in the middle of two or more tasks. This can lead to burnout. Don't forget to make time for yourself. Volunteering should be fun and not a burden. Concentrate on one task at a time so you can see the fruits of your labor.

Be ready to answer questions that nonprofit organizations will have for you.

Be prepared to answer questions. Before you call or visit an organization, sit down with your mom or dad to discuss what your plan of action is. This will help you become better prepared when you speak with your point of contact while discussing your volunteer work.

Parallel your volunteer work to what your goals are.

If your goal is to become a veterinarian, then volunteer your time at a veterinarian's office. Or if you're planning your career toward becoming an arborist, direct your volunteer work toward tree-planting projects. This is a wonderful opportunity to explore your career path.

Volunteering will help your resume and/or college application.

Your volunteer experience will look great on your future job or college application. Many employers and college admission officers are seeking individuals who have a proven record of dedication, desire, and commitment. When applying for a job or college, many times there will be a separate section on the application to list your interests. In this section, you can list your many volunteer experiences.

Think about organizing a committee with your friends.

Volunteering is a great way to bond with your friends. Ask them to join you with a donation drive or fund-raiser.

Give it your all.

Always give 100% of your time, skills, and effort. The organization that you're helping is counting on you.

Don't overlook volunteer opportunities.

We're all familiar with volunteering for churches, hospitals, and libraries. Those are great places to start volunteering. Just remember there are so many more volunteer opportunities to consider. Please take a look at my web site at www.UltimateVolunteer.com for an index of nonprofit organizations that you could donate to, raise money for, or volunteer with.

SECTION ONE

Donation Drives

"Since the days of Greece and Rome when the word 'citizen' was a title of honor, we have often seen more emphasis put on the rights of citizenship than on its responsibilities. And today, as never before in the free world, responsibility is the greatest right of citizenship and service is the greatest of freedom's privileges."—Robert F. Kennedy

It is not fair to ask of others what you are not willing to do yourself.
—*Eleanor Roosevelt*

ACTIVITY 1

Donation Drives in Your Neighborhood

Donate items to a local charity.

Before you begin this donation drive, consider the time of year. I always think about spring cleaning and fall clean-up.

Step 1

How to begin.

Find a local charity to which you'll donate the items. If you find several charities in need, split your donation between organizations. Some local organizations that are found in every city are women's shelter, homeless shelter, and the United Way. Remember to take notes. Finalize all your thoughts and questions. See Sample 1.

Step 2

Set a time frame.

Once you know what organization you will be donating to, decide how long you want to hold the donation drive. Will you accept items for one week, two weeks, or three weeks? I wouldn't recommend holding a donation drive for longer than three weeks, as it might procrastinate their effort to participate. However, if you schedule the drive for too short of a period, then it's possible there will not be enough time for your friends and neighbors to participate. .

Step 3

Map out what streets you will cover in your neighborhood.

Decide on how many streets you will be covering when asking for donations. How many streets are there to cover? How many houses are on each street? One thing to consider is where are you going to store all the items donated? Do you have a large garage? Do you have a vacant room in the house? Make sure you have enough storage space for the anticipated number of donations. The amount of space should reflect the number of homes in your donation area.

Step 4

How will you be packaging the items?

Will you use sturdy boxes? Do you need packaging tape? Would strong yard bags work? Boxes are best because they are free! Free is always good when working a drive. Simply ask a local grocery store manager if you could have available boxes, and when you should collect them. You could even ask if they would be willing to donate packaging tape for your drive. Just remember to send them a thank-you note for the boxes and for the tape if it's donated! They will be more likely to donate again in the future.

Step 5

Call or visit the organization.

It's important to contact the organization. Introduce yourself and explain in full detail what you are wanting to do for them. Be sure to ask them what kind of items is most needed. Give them the dates you plan on having your donation drive and what date you plan on delivering the items. Also, ask if they have a pick-up service. It is possible they will be able to pick up the donated items from your house. If not, make sure you ask for help from a reliable source. You will need help transporting the received items.

Step 6

Notify your neighbors with a letter and be sure to post flyers.

You can use the sample letter and flyer, or you can make your own. Be sure to notify your neighbors at least one week in advance of your donation drive. See Samples 2 and 3.

Step 7

Pick up the donated items from your neighbors' porches.

Make yourself a time schedule of when you will pick up the donated items. If you're using a bike to transport items, you might want to first scout out which neighbors have donated by leaving them on their porch. This way, you can go back home and tell your mom or dad which homes they need to help you with.

Step 8

Keep track.

Keep track of the neighbors who donated. This will also help you keep track of whom you need to send thank-you notes. See Sample 4.

Step 9

Package your items.

Organize the items by categories. Some possible categories are toys, women's clothes, books, shoes, and children's clothes. Now deliver them to the organization!

Step 10

Complete your drive with a thank-you note.

It's time to show your appreciation! Let your neighbors know that their contribution helped others, and that the drive wouldn't have been a success without their support. See Sample 5.

Sample 1—Record Keeping

Charity: Women's Shelter

Spoke with: Jane Mooney Date: March 27th
Phone number: 267-421-8645   Contact time: 1:10 p.m.
Do they have a pick-up service? No
How will you deliver the donated items? Mom's minivan
When will the donation drive begin/end? Sunday, April 16th—Sunday, April 30th
On what day will the items be delivered to the charity? Wednesday, May 3rd
When will you hand out the flyers? Saturday, April, 8th
What kinds of items will you request be donated?
Clean clothes for women and children, shoes, linens, kitchen items, toys, and books.
How many neighborhood blocks will you cover? 3
How many houses are there? 35
What are the names of the streets?
Mockingbird Road, Blue Jay Road, and Cardinal Road

Sample 2—Letter for Donations

Hello my name is Billy Walters, and I live on Mockingbird Road. I am putting together a donation drive in our neighborhood, and I am requesting your help. Would you consider going through your closets, drawers, and cupboards and donate any unwanted items to The Women's Shelter?

I will be picking up items at 4 p.m., everyday, from Sunday, April 16th—Sunday, April 30th. You can leave your items on your porch, and I will come to collect them with my mom or dad. Any donation will be greatly appreciated!

If you have any questions or concerns you can e-mail me at our family's e-mail address: family name@email address, or you may call Jane Mooney at 426-8940. Mrs. Mooney works at the Women's Shelter and is my point of contact.

Thank you in advance for your time and your donation.

Billy Walters

Sample 3—Copy for a Donations Flyer

Participate in a Donation Drive Benefiting The Women's Shelter!

Items will be picked up every Sunday beginning April 16th and lasting through April 30. The drive will include Mockingbird Road, Blue Jay Road, and Cardinal Road. Donated Items can be left on your porch and will be picked up at 4 p.m. each day.

Thank You in advance for your time and contribution.

Sample 4—Keeping Track

Mockingbird Road (By Mailbox Number)

1492	✓ Received Flyer	✓ Donated	✓ Sent Thank-You Note
1493	✓ Received Flyer	✓ Donated	✓ Sent Thank-You Note
1494	✓ Received Flyer	❑ Donated	❑ Sent Thank-You Note
1495	✓Received Flyer	✓ Donated	✓ Sent Thank-You Note
1496	✓Received Flyer	✓ Donated	✓ Sent Thank-You Note

Blue Jay Road (By Mailbox Number)

1628	✓ Received Flyer	✓ Donated	✓ Sent Thank-You Note
1629	✓ Received Flyer	✓ Donated	✓ Sent Thank-You Note
1630	✓ Received Flyer	✓ Donated	✓ Sent Thank-You Note

1631	✓ Received Flyer	✓ Donated	✓ Sent Thank-You Note
1632	✓ Received Flyer	❑ Donated	❑ Sent Thank-You Note
1633	✓ Received Flyer	✓ Donated	✓ Sent Thank-You Note
1634	✓ Received Flyer	✓ Donated	✓ Sent Thank-You Note

Cardinal Road (By Mailbox Number)

1802	✓ Received Flyer	✓ Donated	✓ Sent Thank-You Note
1803	✓ Received Flyer	❑ Donated	❑ Sent Thank-You Note
1804	✓ Received Flyer	✓ Donated	✓ Sent Thank-You Note
1805	✓ Received Flyer	❑ Donated	❑ Sent Thank-You Note
1806	✓ Received Flyer	✓ Donated	✓ Sent Thank-You Note

Sample 5—Thank-You Note

Mr. and Mrs. Randall,

I want to thank you so much for participating in my donation drive. Not only have you helped me accomplish my goal of collecting 25 boxes of donated items, but you have helped so many people in this cause.

Thank you again,

Billy Walters

Charity sees the need, not the cause.—German Proverb

Activity 2

School Supply Drive

Donate the supplies to a school that's in need.

This donation drive is especially fun. You will find that most people and children will donate to your cause. School supplies are relatively afford-able, so many people can participate. The beginning and middle of the school year are good times to have this drive.

Step 1

How to begin.

Find a school or a charity to which you would like to donate your school supplies to. You can probably ask your school district's office about the need for school supplies at local schools in the area. If you wish to donate the school supplies to a third-world country, find a charity that will help you with your cause. Please refer to www.UltimateVolunteer.com for a list of nonprofit organizations. Also, please keep in mind that if you want to ship them somewhere, you'll have to figure out the cost of the shipment. Who will pay for the shipping? Take notes. See Sample 1.

Step 2

Plan a time frame.

When does school begin? January is also a time when parents and students replenish school supplies. Parents and students usually begin buying their school supplies 2-3 weeks ahead of school start. The weekends are always big shopping days. Plan two fun weekends to set up a table at a store. If the drive is at your school, try to make it within the first month after school has started.

Step 3

Map out where you plan on holding your donation drive.

Where? What date(s)? What weekend(s)? For how long? You can have the drive at a local store that's popular in your area. Get permission to set up a table outside of the store to receive any donations. You can ask the store manager to set up a display at the entrance of the store to make it more convenient for people who wish to donate to pick up any supplies they wish in the store. If you plan on a drive at school, set up a display at the entrance of the school. Make sure you have plenty of boxes to support the amount of donations given by fellow students. Plan on having the drive at the beginning of the school year or a couple weeks before winter or midyear break.

Step 4

How will you be packaging the items?

Here's what you may need. Sturdy boxes? Plastic bins? Packaging tape? Poster boards? Paper?

Step 5

Call the store manager or visit the store manager. Call the principal or visit the principal of your school.

Make the phone call or make a visit to propose your intention of the drive. Suggest when you want to do the school supply drive. Is that a good time for them? For the school? Tell them how you wish to advertise your school-wide drive. Who will be helping you? Can the PTA get involved with your school supply drive?

Step 6

Advertise your school supply donation drive.

How will you get the word out? If you use your school as a platform, you might want to put a display board out with facts about your cause. See Sample 2. Give your fellow students a week's time to prepare for the donation. Maybe set up an extra display board that's labeled as a helping hand board to post names of students who have helped you with your cause. See Sample 3.

If you're setting up a table at a local store, you don't need to advertise. You'll get the traffic you need to have a successful school supply drive from their customers. However, you'll need a couple of advertising posters to express the need of these supplies.

Step 7

(Only if you're using your school as a platform for your school supply donation drive)

How often will you collect your donated supplies?

Daily? Weekly? I would suggest you package the supplies at school. Leave the packaged boxes at school, with a sign that reads, "Going to Harvest Elementary" for example. This is to show a visual of all your efforts and your students' efforts toward the cause.

Step 8

Keep track.

Take inventory of how many items of each school supply has been donated. This information will help the receiving school to determine how they will divide them to students, grades, or classes. See Sample 4.

Step 9

Send them off!

As soon as the school supply drive is over, pack your items according to weight and item. Find sturdy boxes to pack them in and label the boxes with the school supply item.

Step 10

Write and send your thank-you notes.

Thank everyone involved. Write a thank-you note to the store manager or to your principal. Thank your fellow students by posting a display board at the entrance of the school thanking them for all their efforts. Give them an exact amount of school supplies donated. See Sample 5.

Sample 1—Record Keeping

Charity: Harvest District Schools

Spoke with: Dr. Morris, Principal   Date: July 15th
Phone number: 563-9873 Contact time: 9:00 a.m.
Can I have the donation drive from September 15—30? Yes
Who will help to volunteer with your drive? My Mom and my friend Macy
What kinds of items will be donated? Crayons, glue, paper, scissors, rulers, pens, pencils, markers, etc.

How many children are at your school? 750 students

Who will help you with your display boards? My mom and my friend Macy

Have you contacted the principals at the schools you wish to donate these school supplies to? Yes, all of them.

When would be a good time to deliver these supplies? Once the donation drive is over, I will be able to deliver them to the main office.

Sample 2—Advertising Flyer

Did you know that more than 15,000 children in our area live in poverty? Their families cannot afford school supplies. Please help me make a difference in their lives.

The following supplies are needed by Grades:

K—2	3—6	7—12
backpack	backpack	backpack
crayons	crayons	pens
glue	glue	pencils
Rounded scissors	Pointed scissors	Highlighter
Wide-ruled paper	Wide-ruled paper	red correcting pens
pencils	pencils	markers
wide-tip markers	markers	pointed scissors
pocket folder	binder	binder
ruler	ruler	ruler
eraser	eraser	college-ruled paper
map pencils	map pencils	map pencils
pens	notebook paper	
wide-ruled spiral	calculator	

Sample 3—Helping Hand

For your helping hand display board, you can trace your hand onto blank sheets of paper and write the students' names that donated school supplies.

Cut out and place on your helping hand display board

Sample 4—Keeping Track

Number of each item donated:

Crayons: 87

Glue: 95

Rulers: 92

Pens: 90

Packs of pencils: 90

Map pencils: 76

Scissors: 68

Markers: 90

Folders: 93

Binders: 86

Packs of paper: 172

Highlighters: 89

Backpacks: 46

Sample 5—Thank-You Note

Dr. Morris,

Thank you very much for supporting my school supply donation drive. It was such a success! Your approval and support has helped many children who are without school supplies. I hope to work with you and my fellow students on future donation drives.

Thank you,

Becky Freeland

The manner of giving is worth more than the gift.
—Pierre Corneille, Le Menteur

Activity 3

Throw a Toy Donation Party

Have your guests bring a wrapped toy for a needy child.

This donation drive is so much fun. You can have it anytime of the year and for any occasion.

Step 1

How to begin.

Find a charity to which you can donate the toys. Some organizations that are found in every city are Toys for Tots and a local children's hospital. To find your local contact person for Toys for Tots, go to www.toysfortots.org.

Step 2

Call the organization or visit the organization.

Call or visit the organization to which you will donate your toys. Make sure you take plenty of notes and ask lots of questions. Find out if they have a list of desired toys and what age-appropriate toys they need. Take notes! See Sample 1.

Step 3

Plan a time frame.

When do you want to throw your toy donation party? What time of year? What day? What will be your theme? My favorite time of year is the fall. You could always have a social gathering in the month of October and have a costume theme party. That's always fun! Perhaps you could use your own birthday as a platform to throw a party and donate all your presents to a charity for kids. In your invitation, you could request your guests to bring a boy or girl wrapped present. It's up to you . . . have fun with it!

Step 4

How big of a party do you want to have? Who will you invite?

Depending on where you have your party depends on how many people you can invite. Will you have your party at your house? At a local park? Will you have a pool party? A garage party? Ask your parent(s) to help you make this decision. They play a big role in this donation drive. Brainstorm ideas and put forth your plan.

Step 5

How will you be delivering the toys?

It is most likely that you will have to deliver the toys to the nonprofit organization. Make sure you set up a day and time to deliver them with the person you have coordinated with. Ask your mom or dad to help you deliver the toys and thank them for all their help. Finalize all your thoughts for your toy drive.

Step 6

Send out your party invitations.

Make sure you invite all your friends! Be specific of the type of birthday party you're having. Give the date and time along with which organization you're donating your birthday gifts. See Sample 2.

Step 7

Keep track.

Make sure you keep track of the gifts that are brought to the party. Also, as your guests bring their gift, you can put a number on the gift and give out a different number to each person so that everyone participates when it's time to unwrap presents. As each person unwraps a donated toy, you can ask your guest, who brought that present, to stand up and tell everyone why he or she decided on that gift. It makes the most out of the generous donation your guest made. See Sample 3.

Step 8

Make a toast.

Before your birthday party has ended, make a toast. Thank everyone for attending your birthday party and for the gifts that were given. Express the importance of your chosen organization and just how much the organization helps children.

Step 9

Pack them up!

Because toys are nicely packaged, you will probably only need sturdy plastic bags to transport them. You can also help by categorizing the toys by boy/girl toys and possibly age group.

Step 10

Follow up with thank-you notes.

Make sure you thank all of your friends for the toy they brought to your toy donation party. Also, make sure you mention the name of the toy they brought and how it will guarantee a smile on a child's face. See Sample 4.

Sample 1—Record Keeping

Charity: Toys for Tots

Spoke with: Jaime Cantu   Date: October 8th

Phone number 734-7061   Contact time: 11:30 a.m.

Do they have a pick-up service? No

How will you deliver the toys? Dad will drive me to the drop-off location.

When will you have the party? On my birthday, October 27th.

When will you drop off the toys? On November 2nd

When will you send out your invitations? Two weeks before my party, October 14th.

What kinds of toys will you ask your guests to donate? Any kind of boy or girl toy of their choice.

How many guests will you invite: 22 friends

Where will you have your party? In my parents' garage.

What is the theme of your party? I will be having a costume birthday party.

Who will you invite?

1. Kari	12. Lori
2. Sarah	13. Heidi
3. Kevin	14. James
4. Joy	15. Carter
5. Lenni	16. Ava
6. Andy	17. Samuel
7. Henry	18. Ryder
8. Maria	19. Patricia

9. Janice   20. Ryan
10. Jose   21. Chris
11. Kelsey   22. Hector

Sample 2—Party Invitation

You're Invited to my Costume Birthday Party!
On Friday, October 27th at 7 o'clock
I will be donating all my birthday presents to The Toys for Tots Foundation
Please bring a wrapped boy or girl present to the party and be prepared to
participate in unwrapping a present.
See You There!

Sample 3—Keeping Track

Guest	Donated Toy	Sent Thank-You Note
Kari	stuffed monkey	✓
Hector	football	✓
Ava	building blocks	✓
Joy	baby doll	✓
Henry	Lincoln Logs	✓
Andy	baseball bat and ball	❑
Sarah	Barbie doll	✓
Kevin	basketball	❑
Maria	Monopoly game	❑
James	model car	❑
Patricia	Barbie doll	✓
Kelsey	puzzle	✓
Jose	Play-dough	✓
Heidi	Strawberry Shortcake doll	❑
Lori	Etch-a-Sketch	✓
Janice	baby doll	✓
Ryan	Thomas the Train	✓
Samuel	Little People School Bus	✓
Chris	play car	✓
Carter	play make-up	❑
Ryder	stuffed teddy bear	✓

Sample 4—Thank-You Note

Patricia,

Thank you so much for coming to my birthday party and participating by donating a beautiful Barbie Doll to the Toys for Tots Foundation. I loved the fact that you purchased the Barbie Doll because it's your favorite doll at home. I know your donation will bring a big smile to a child in need.

Your friend,

Stacey

P.S. I loved your costume.

Reading is to the mind what exercise is to the body.
—Richard Steele, Tatler, 1710

Activity 4

Book Drive for Your Local Library

This donation drive could be a wonderful project conducted during the summer months. During the summer, the library has lots of reading programs for kids and adults alike. Get involved with making a difference for your local library.

Step 1

How to begin.

Find a local library that needs help with its supply of books. Ask for a list of desired and or needed books. Take a tour of the library and make a checklist of how many sections they have. Possibly set a goal for yourself to have a certain amount of books donated to each section of the library.

Step 2

Plan a time frame.

How long will you have your book drive? One week? Two weeks? Three weeks? I recommend having your book drive for at least two full weeks.

Step 3

Where will you be holding your donation book drive?

You can hold your donation book drive outside a local bookstore, but make sure you get permission from the store manager. Explain what you're trying to do for your local library. Let the manager know that this could also be an incentive for his or her bookstore. Ask the manager to order the books that are on the desired book list to make sure they are readily available for purchase. Also, ask the manager to set up a display for your book drive. Have the manager stock all the books you need for your library.

Step 4

How will you be packaging the books?

You will definitely need sturdy boxes for your book drive. Ask the bookstore if they have any to spare. You could also ask the local grocery store.

Step 5

Call the organization or visit the organization.

Make sure you make contact with the head librarian to introduce yourself. Make sure you express why this project is important to you. Ask the head librarian to give you a tour of the library and find out what books are needed.

Step 6

Record keeping.

Take notes. Finalize all your thoughts for your donation drive. See Sample 1.

Step 7

Advertise.

Post flyers at the library and at the bookstore. Make sure you make copies of the desired books needed for the library. Keep a homemade drop box at the bookstore for the times you're not there to collect them. Remember to remove all the flyers after your event. See Sample 2.

Step 8

Keeping track.

Make sure to keep track of what books have been donated. Keep track of the dates you collect them and the inventory of your count by book classification. See Sample 3.

Step 9

Pack them up!

Deliver the books. Maybe even ask to help inventory the books and place them on the shelf.

Step 10

Thank everyone involved.

Be sure to thank the library and the bookstore that helped make your book drive a successful one! See Sample 4.

Sample 1—Record Keeping

Charity: Richardson Library

Spoke with: Kimberly Williams, Librarian   Date: May 4th
Phone number: 243-5123 Contact time: 2:30 p.m.
Do they have a pick-up service: No
How will you be delivering the donated books? Mom will help me deliver them.
When will you have your book drive? June 15—July 1
When will you deliver the books? At the end of my book drive.
What kinds of books will you ask people to donate?
I will encourage people to purchase books from my desired book list, but they can purchase any fiction or nonfiction books.
Where will you hold your book drive: At Barnes and Nobles book store
Spoke with: Keith Adams Title: Store Manager   Date: May 10th
Phone number: 243-0756 Time: 11:30 a.m.

Sample 2—Desired Book List

Adult Nonfiction

The Ethics of Identity by Kwame Appiah
Conspiracy of Fools: A True Story by Kurt Eichenwald
The Works: Anatomy of a City by Kate Ascher
True Story: Murder, Memoir, Mea Culpa by Michael Finkel
Orphans by Charles D'Ambrosio

Adult Fiction

The History of Love: A Novel by Nicole Krause
Never Let Me Go by Kazuo Ishiguro
Veronica: A Novel by Mary Gaitskill
No Country for Old Men by Cormac McCarthy

Children's Books

Diary of a Spider by Doreen Cronin
Clara and Asha by Eric Rohmann
Rosa by Nikki Giovanni
Little Pea by Amy Krouse Rosenthal

Bad Baby by Ross MacDonald
PreHistoric Actual Size by Steve Jenkins
Anne Frank by Josephine Poole
Zen Shorts by Jon J. Muth

Mystery and Thriller

Two Trains Running by Andrew Vachss
Six Bad Things by Charlie Huston
Cinnamon Kiss by Walter Mosley
Eleven on Top by Janet Evanovich
The Broker by John Grisham

Science Fiction and Fantasy

The Algebraist by Iain M. Banks
Accelerando by Charles Stross
Olympos by Dan Simmons

Romance

A Breath of Snow and Ashes by Diana Gabaldon
It's in His Kiss by Julia Quinn
The Trouble with Valentine's Day by Rachel Gibson
Wait Until Midnight by Amanda Quick
Dark Secret by Christine Feehan

Magazines Subscriptions	*Newspapers Subscriptions*
National Geographic	USA Today
People	New York Post
Popular Science	Washington Post
Bon Appetit	
Discover	

Sample 3—Keeping Track

	6/16	6/18	6/20	6/22	6/24	6/26	6/28	7/1	Total
Adult NF	7	12	5	6	5	9	11	14	69
Adult F	11	6	9	6	14	8	5	8	67
Children's	7	6	7	10	11	9	9	5	64
Mystery	5	9	4	6	9	4	8	5	50
Romance	3	5	6	7	6	3	7	4	41
Magazines	5	7	4	7	8	5	3	6	45

Newspapers	3	2	2	1	0	3	1	4	16
Sci-fi	6	3	5	7	8	5	3	6	43
Total:									395

Sample 4—Thank-You Note

Note to the Librarian:

Ms. Kimberly Williams,
Thank you so much for assisting me with a list of desired books needed for your library. The book drive was a success! Also, thank you for showing me the process of how a library operates.
Sincerely,

Casey James

Note to the Bookstore Manager:

Mr. Keith Adams,
Thank you very much for allowing me to set up a table outside your store. My book drive was such a success. Your staff was so generous! Their help to locate many of the books on my book-desired list was so great. It made many of the book donations easy and smooth.
Thank you again,

Casey James

Every tooth in a man's head is more valuable than a diamond.
—Miguel de Cervantes, Don Quixote

Activity 5

Toothbrush, Toothpaste, and Dental Floss Donation Drive

Donate the products to people that are in need.
This activity is great for anytime of the year. It's hard to imagine that there are so many people that go without these basic items.

Step 1

How to begin.

Find an organization to which you can send these items. Also, make contact with the organization to which you wish to donate. Find out what their needs are. What supplies are needed? Here are some organizations that are found in every city: Head Start Programs, Healthy Start, pediatric health centers, community health fairs. You can get online support such as www.kidssmiles.org. Take notes. See Sample 1.

Step 2

Plan a time frame.

Once you know what organization you will be donating to, be sure to set a time frame. Give yourself enough time to write letters to dentist offices or put up advertising at your school or at a local grocery store.

Step 3

How will you be packaging the items?

You can use plastic bags for the floss and toothpaste, but you will need boxes for the toothpaste because it is heavier than the other items. Get the boxes from your local supermarket . . . they're free.

Step 4

Keep track.

Map out what dentist offices you are going to request materials from, or at what store you can advertise. Make a list of organizations, offices, and stores that are near your home. See Sample 2.

Step 5

Make contact.

Call or visit the dentist offices from which you wish to get donations. Also, call the stores and school on your list to get permission for your donation boxes to be placed.

Step 6

Advertise your campaign.

Make a flyer for your donation drive. Also, consider making a morning announcement at school to inform your school mates about the drive. Remember to remove all the flyers after your event. See Sample 3.

Step 7

Pick them up!

Pick up the donated supplies from all the dentist offices, school, or grocery stores. Take inventory from each office and place of business. See Sample 4.

Step 8

Deliver the items!

Deliver the toothbrushes, toothpaste, and dental floss. Remember to give the inventory list to your contact person.

Step 9

Keep a journal.

Write down all your thoughts and experiences of your dental hygiene donation drive. What did you like most about this donation drive? Did you make any new friends?

Step 10

Follow up!

Remember to thank everyone involved. Thank the dentist offices for their generous donations. Also, thank the stores and school that helped you raised so many dental hygiene products. See Sample 5.

Sample 1—Record Keeping

Charity: Healthy Start (Local Branch)

Spoke with: Katy Goode   Date: July 16th

Phone number: 467-2825 Contact time: 2:10 p.m.

Web site: www.healthy-start.com

What is needed for the Healthy Start program? Toothpaste, toothbrushes, and floss

Do they have a pick-up service? No

Will you have to deliver the donated Items? Yes

How will you deliver the donated items? Dad will take me to the Healthy Start office.

When will the donation drive begin? August 12—September 10, 2007

On what day will you be delivering the donated items to Healthy Start? September 15, 2007

Who is your focus group from which to get donated items?

Local dentists', neighbors, family members, school mates, and local grocery stores.

How many dentist offices will you cover? 29

What grocery stores will you campaign at? Crosby Supermarket and Freeland Grocery Store

What school will you campaign at? Gentry Middle School

Sample 2—Keeping Track

Dentist Offices:

Dentist	Spoke with:	Donate (Yes/No)
Orlando Apollo, L DDS	Helen Stewart	Yes
Kimberly Ambrose, L DDS	Monica Lee	Yes
Sarah Anderson, D DDS	Terry Williams	Yes
Lewis Barnes, L DDS	Brenda Thomas	Yes
Gary Barcliffe, D DDS	Mary Peters	Yes
Andrew Carroll, D DDS	Lilly Monroe	Yes
Jennifer Cannon, L DDS	Kelly Garcia	Yes
Erica Daily, L DDS	Veronica Hale	Yes
Donald Fowler, D DDS	Michelle Johnson	Yes
Maria Garza, L DDS	Lupe Fernandez	Yes
Christian Giles, L DDS	Joanne Moore	Yes

Patrick Holland, L DDS	Micky Jordan	Yes
J. K. James, D DDS	Trina Upmale	Yes
Peter McDonald, D DDS	Yolanda Williams	Yes
Ingrid Montgomery, L DDS	Gabrielle Solis	Yes
Silvia Neal, D DDS	Heather Kennedy	Yes

Grocery Stores:

| Crosby Supermarket | Linda Morrison | Can set up box |
| Freeland Grocery Store | Mark Bruce | Can set up box |

School:

| Gentry Middle School | Melinda Campbell, Principal | Can set up box |

Sample 3—Advertisement Flyer

Participate in a Donation Drive Benefiting
Healthy Start
www.healthy-start.com
Items needed are: Toothpaste, Tooth Brushes and Dental Floss
Items will be collected throughout the weeks of:
August 12—September 10, 2007
Donated Items Can Be Dropped In This Box.
Thank You in Advance for your Donation.

Sample 4—Inventory List

Office/Organization	Tooth paste	Tooths brushes	Floss	Total
Orlando Apollo, L DDS	25	25	25	75
Kimberly Ambrose, L DDS	40	40	40	120
Sarah Anderson, D DDS	50	50	50	150
Lewis Barnes, L DDS	50	50	50	150
Gary Barcliffe, D DDS	50	50	50	150
Andrew Carroll, D DDS	25	25	25	75
Jennifer Cannon, L DDS	25	25	25	75
Erica Daily, L DDS	50	50	50	150
Donald Fowler, D DDS	20	20	20	60
Maria Garza, L DDS	25	25	25	75
Christian Giles, L DDS	25	25	25	75

Patrick Holland, L DDS	25	25	25	75
J. K. James, D DDS	50	50	50	150
Peter McDonald, D DDS	25	25	25	75
Ingrid Montgomery, L DDS	25	25	25	75
Silvia Neal, D DDS	25	25	25	75

Sample 5—Thank-You Note

Dr. Neal and Staff,

I want to thank you for participating in my donation drive. So many people will benefit from all the dental supplies that you donated. Your donation helped me collect 1,159 toothbrushes, 1,160 tubes of toothpaste, and 605 containers of dental floss.

Thank you again,

Jane Hewitt

No one is more cherished in this world than someone who lightens the burden of another.—Author Unknown

Activity 6

Scavenger Hunt Donation Drive

This donation drive requires adult supervision at all time. It is also very fun.

Step 1

How to begin.

Find a local charity to which you can donate the items. Call or visit the organization. Introduce yourself and tell them why you chose their organization. Let them know how you plan on collecting donated items. Request a list of items that are desired. Also, who will you invite? You can select three teams of three persons to conduct your scavenger hunt. Remember each team needs adult supervision. Take lots of notes. See Sample 1.

Step 2

Plan a time frame.

When will you have your scavenger hunt? What time of day? I suggest having it on a Saturday starting at 6 p.m. The fun part about a scavenger hunt is that it's usually conducted in the evening. Also, make sure you use your time well. Time management is very important with this drive because once it starts getting too late it's not polite to disturb your neighbors or a neighborhood. Make a plan of action of how many houses each team will cover and approximately how long it will take to cover each block.

Step 3

Map out what blocks you will be covering in your neighborhood.

Make sure you have equal amount of neighborhoods and equal amount of houses for each team.

Step 4

Packaging the items.

Try to get free boxes from grocery store. If you use plastic bags, make sure they're sturdy.

Step 5

Scavenger hunt list.

Make a list for the scavenger hunt. Be sure to list items that are found in most homes. See Sample 2.

Step 6

Notify the houses.

Notify the people that live on the blocks you want to cover. Simply put a letter or a flyer in their box. Remember not to give them the scavenger hunt list of items! See Samples 3 & 4.

Step 7

Keep track.

Keep track of who donated and who didn't. This is a great way to keep track of to who you need to send a thank-you note. See Sample 5.

Step 8

Keep a journal.

Did you have a fun hosting your scavenger hunt donation drive? Journal your experience!

Step 9

Pack up the items!

Pack the items accordingly. It would be nice to pack the items by category, that is, women's clothing, household goods, or linens.

Step 10

Write your thank-you notes.

Thank everyone who participated with your scavenger hunt. Thank your friends and all the chaperones involved. See Sample 6.

Sample 1—Record Keeping

Charity: United Way

Spoke with: Henry Carroll Date: September 27th
Phone number: 987-4013 Contact time: 10:05 a.m.
Do they have pick-up service? Yes
How will they deliver the items? N/A
When will they pick up the items donated? Monday, October 17th at 4 p.m.
When will you hand out the letters or flyers? Saturday, October 8th
What kinds of items will you request be donated?
Electronics, Kitchen Appliances, Cookware, Dishes, Linen, and Wardrobe
How many neighborhood blocks will you cover? 9 blocks
How many houses are there? 386 houses/44 houses on each block
What are the names of the streets? Foster Street, Monroe Street, Garrett
Street, Bosley Street, Paisley Street, Lowell Street, Renta Street, Hershey
Street and Hewitt Street
Team 1 Covers: Foster, Monroe, and Garrett Street
Team 2 Covers: Bosley, Paisley, and Lowell Street
Team 3 Covers: Renta, Hershey, and Hewitt Street
What will you need for each team: 1 adult chaperone for each team, 1 car
for each team, flashlights, or belt reflectors

Sample 2—Scavenger Hunt List

Household Items

Electronics

Computer	200 pts
Television	175 pts
Radio	150 pts
Stereo	150 pts
VCR	125 pts
DVD player	125 pts
IPOD	100 pts

Dishes

Plates	80 pts
Bowls	80 pts
Coffee cups	80 pts
Saucers	80 pts
Drinking glasses	80 pts
Desert plates	80 pts

Forks	75 pts
Spoons	75 pts
Knives	75 pts
Butter knives	75 pts
Spatula	75 pts
Serving bowl	90 pts
Serving platter	90 pts

Appliances

Microwave	150 pts
Blender	140 pts
Toaster	135 pts
Mixer	135 pts
Coffee maker	135 pts
Waffle maker	135 pts
Crock Pot	135 pts
Juicer	135 pts

Cookware

Pot	100 pts
Pan	100 pts
Skillet	100 pts

Linens

Towel	75 pts
Hand towel	70 pts
Wash cloth	65 pts
Fitted sheets	75 pts
Flat sheets	75 pts
Pillow cases	70 pts
Blankets	100 pts

Wardrobe

Coat	100 pts
Shoes	95 pts
Pants	95 pts
Shirt	95 pts
Sweater	95 pts
T-Shirt	85 pts

Socks	85 pts
Gloves	85 pts
Scarf	85 pts
Blouse	95 pts
Belt	85 pts
Tie	85 pts

The team with the most points has bragging rights.
Remember that this competition is benefiting others . . . you are all winners.

Sample 3—Notification Letter

Hewitt Street Resident,
Hi. My name is Nancy Walsh. My friends and I are having a scavenger hunt donation drive, Saturday, March 3rd, beginning at 6 p.m. I'm asking for your participation in our cause to help the men, women, and children of our community, through the United Way, build a brighter future by giving them a helping hand with donated household items. If you have any questions concerning this donation drive please contact my parents at: ParentsOfNancyWalsh@familyemail.com or you may contact Henry Carroll, from the United Way, at HenryCarroll@HenryCarroll.com with any questions concerning our donation drive.
Thank you,

Nancy Walsh

Sample 4—Advertisement Flyer

Participate in our Scavenger Hunt
Donation Drive Benefiting The United Way
Saturday, March 3rd Beginning at 6 p.m.
We are covering the following streets:
Foster Street, Monroe Street, Garrett Street, Bosley Street, Paisley Street, Lowell Street, Renta Street, Hershey Street, and Hewitt Street
Any unwanted household items will be much appreciated.
Thank you,
Nancy Walsh

Sample 5—Keeping Track

Foster Street

House #	Donated	Thank-You Note Sent
903	✓	✓
904	✓	✓
905		
905		
906	✓	✓
907		
908	✓	✓
909	✓	
910	✓	
911		
912	✓	
913		

Make similar lists for the other streets in your scavenger hunt.

Sample 6—Thank-You Note

Resident,

Thank you so much for participating in my Scavenger Hunt Donation Drive. My friends and I had so much fun interacting with all of the residents. I'm amazed with all the kindness and generosity we received. We truly had a successful night.

Thank you again,

Nancy Walsh

*"I've got big shoes to fill. This is my chance to do something.
I have to seize the moment."—Andrew Jackson*

Activity 7

Sock and Shoe Donation Drive

This drive is great because who doesn't like their shoes? Shoes have been making statements for a long time. Can you imagine not having any shoes or having shoes that do not fit right? Once a year the Germans put their unwanted shoes out in a basket, to be picked up by the city, for those that are in need. Isn't that a wonderful tradition?

Step 1

Make contact.

Find a local or national charity to which you can donate the socks and shoes. Find out what their needs are. Here are some local charities found in every city: women's shelter and homeless shelter. You can also donate them to a national organization such as: Angel Care (Children's Angel Care International). Call or visit the organization you wish to donate the socks and shoes. Introduce yourself. Let them know what you're trying to accomplish, why it's important to you, and how you will try to achieve your goal. Write the name of the person or persons you spoke with. See Sample 1.

Step 2

Plan a time frame.

Once you find the organization you wish to donate the socks and shoes to, plan a time frame that's right for you. Decide for how long you want to hold your donation drive.

Step 3

Where will you find assistance?

Who will you ask to donate these items? Will you try to start a tradition in your community? Will you ask shoe stores such as Payless or Wal-Mart if they could donate any shoes to your cause? Could you set a table outside a local Payless store to receive any donated shoes? I would suggest that you try to make it as simple as possible. Either put a flyer in your community's mailbox asking them to put any unwanted shoes out on their porch or get permission to set a table outside a popular shoe store.

Step 4

How will you be packaging the items?

If your charity is a local charity, find out if they have a pick-up service. If they don't, heavy-duty trash bags would work great for the socks and shoes collected. If you're sending the shoes to a national charity, find out where you need to send them, and who the contact person is.

Step 5

Advertise your donation drive.

How are you going to advertise your drive? Will you use flyers, poster boards, or letters? However you do it, make sure your message is clear. See Sample 2.

Step 6

Supply list.

Make a list of supplies you'll need for your weekend drive. See Sample 3.

Step 7

Keep track.

Remember to always keep track of who donated or who helped you with your drive. See Sample 4.

Step 8

Keep a journal.

Write your thoughts and feelings about your experiences from your donation drive. Did you have a great experience? Did you make any new friends?

Step 9

Send them off!

Whether you send them to an organization by package or carrying them in a sturdy bag to the organization, you'll want to always make it easy for the receiver. There are some easy ways to do this. You can sort the shoes by gender or by size, and you can tie the shoes together with their shoelaces. You could also get a rubber band and wrap it around each pair of shoes so they won't lose their partner. Do this with the socks as well.

Step 10

Thank everyone.

This step is really important because without these people helping you with your drive, your drive wouldn't be a success. Also, remember to thank your parents. They love you very much and have worked very hard to help make your drive such a success. See Sample 5.

Sample 1—Record Keeping

Charity: Angel Care (Children's Angel Care International)

Spoke with: Holly Douglas Date: October 4th
Phone number: 326-0385 Contact time: 9:30 a.m.
Do they have pick-up service? No
How will you deliver the items? Will send them in the mail.
What address will you send the socks and shoes? Angel Care, P.O. Box 600370, San Diego, CA 92160-0370
When will you hand out the letters or flyers? Saturday, October 8th
What kinds of items will you request be donated?
Socks and Shoes for all ages

Manager at Payless: Lolly Franco
Date: October 4th Contact time: 11:15 a.m.
Will they donate socks and shoes? Yes
Can you set up a table outside store? Yes
What day? Saturday, October 15th
Time: 10:00 a.m.–5:00 p.m.

Manager at Wal-Mart: Kirby Day
Date: October 4th Contact time: 11:45 a.m.
Will they donate socks and shoes? Yes
Can you set up a table outside store? Yes
What day? Saturday, October 21st

Time: 10:00 a.m.—5:00 p.m.

Sample 2—Advertisement Flyer

Participate in a Donation Drive Benefiting

Angel Care

www.angelcare.org

I am requesting for any unwanted socks or shoes for my drive. Socks and Shoes will be picked up every Saturday starting from November 4th through November 18th. Donated socks and shoes can be left on your porch and will be picked up after 12 p.m.

If you have any questions or concerns, please contact my family e-mail address at familyemail@familyemail.com

Thank You in Advance.

Sample 3—Supply List

Table

(2) Chairs

Flyers to hand out with information about Angel Care and what kind of donation you're asking.

Sandwiches (for lunch)

Sample 4—Keeping Track

Organization or Donating Persons	Number of Shoes Donated?	Number of Socks Donated?	Thank-You Note Sent?
Payless Shoe Store	45	45	Yes
Wal-Mart	25	25	Yes
Donations outside of Payless	12	18	Thanked as they donated
Donations outside of Wal-Mart	8	37	Thanked as they donated
Donations made from Holly Lane	23	52	Yes. As I picked up
Donations made from Tooley Lane	11	18	Yes. As I picked up
Donations made from Jolly Lane	33	64	Yes. As I picked up
Donations made	56	72	Yes. As I

from Bonnie Lane   picked up
TOTALS   213   331

Sample 5—Thank-You Note

Thank-you note to PayLess and Wal-Mart:

Dear _____,
Thank you very much for donating socks and shoes toward my sock and shoe donation drive benefiting Angel Care. I was able to collect _____ shoes and _____ socks. That amount includes the additional socks and shoes donated by your customers. It was a success! I couldn't have done it without you and your company.
Thank you,

Lori Neilson

Generic thank-you note to resident neighbors. (You can put this letter or note in their mailbox as you pick up socks and shoes from their porch.)
Dear Resident,
Thank you very much for donating your socks and shoes toward my drive benefiting Angel Care. You and your neighbors have made a huge contribution!
My drive wouldn't have been such a success without your help.
Thank you,

Lori Neilson

Of all the senses, sight must be the most delightful.—Helen Keller

Activity 8

Eyeglass Donation Drive

This donation drive can be ongoing, conducted throughout the year.

Step 1

Make contact.

Find a local or national charity to donate the eyeglasses. Find out what their needs are. Contact the organization. Introduce yourself and explain in full detail how you're interested in helping with the collection of eyeglasses for their organization. Let them know that your volunteer work to collect eyeglasses will be ongoing. See Sample 1.

Here are two nonprofit organizations that collect eyeglasses: The Lion's Club is a local organization found in almost every city. If you don't have a Lion's Club, you can find one near your city by going to their web site at www.lionsclubs.org.

Unite For Sight is a national nonprofit organization with which I've volunteered with. You can read more about this organization by visiting their web site at: www.uniteforsight.org

Step 2

Plan a time frame.

When will you have your eyeglass drive? How long will you campaign? You should set a goal of how many eyeglasses you want to collect before you send them to an organization of choice. You can also have an ongoing campaign. You can make drop boxes for each target location and set them there permanently—checking them weekly, biweekly, or monthly. This way you can elect yourself a permanent ambassador for your organization of choice.

Step 3

Map out where you plan on holding your donation drive.

Who will you ask to donate eyeglasses? How will you conduct your donation drive? I suggest that you make drop-off boxes to place at many locations. Decorate your boxes and cut out a hole at the top of the box. Also, on the box, list to what organization the eyeglasses will be donated. Give some information about the area that's in need of the eyeglasses. See Samples 2 and 3.

Step 4

Deliver the drop-off boxes.

As you deliver the boxes, find a visible location. Get permission for this location. Remember to add your name and phone number or e-mail address to the bottom of the box, just in case the organization needs to contact you.

Step 5

Advertise.

Call your local news or radio station and ask if you could be interviewed to express the need of used and new prescription eyeglasses and sunglasses. Give the media the drop-off locations of your boxes. Your effort to let your community know may pay off for your eyeglass donation drive.

Step 6

Keeping track.

Keep track of all the organizations you have a drop-off box. See Sample 4.

Step 7

How will you be packaging the items?.

Mailing the eyeglasses you collect to the organization for donation would be very inexpensive. Eyeglasses are very light in weight and are very small. You could probably fit approximately 30-35 pairs of eyeglasses in a shoebox.

Step 8

Keep a journal.

Write down all your thoughts about experiences from your eyeglass donation drive. Are you enjoying your campaign?

Step 9

Send them off!

Before you send off the eyeglasses be sure to clean them. Be sure to clean the lenses with the proper cloth so that you don't scratch them. Put a card in the box and explain how much it meant to you to be able to participate in this drive.

Step 10

Thank everyone.

Thank the offices that helped you collect your eyeglasses. See Sample 5.

Sample 1—Record Keeping

Organization: Unite for Sight

Spoke with: Jennifer Stapleton   Date: May 4th
Phone number: 658-6092 Contact time: 11:30 a.m.
E-mail: Jennifer.Stapleton@uniteforsight.org
What are you collecting?
Reading eyeglasses, prescription eyeglasses, and sunglasses for all ages
Where will the eyeglasses be sent?
To rural parts of Africa and China
When are you planning your eyeglass drive?
October 1st—December 31st
How many do you have to collect before you send them off?
100—200 eyeglasses
Who will you ask?
Family, friends, neighbors, mom and dad's coworkers, and eye doctor's offices

Sample 2—Advertising Flyer

Eyeglass Donation Drive Benefiting Unite For Sight
Reading Eyeglasses, Prescription Eyeglasses, and Sunglasses are needed for all ages
Note: The Lion's Club and Unite for Sight have flyers kits that you can use with which to advertise.

Sample 3—List of Needed Supplies

Now you need to make drop boxes for your eyeglass donation drive. Here's what you need:

Boxes with tops.

Paper to cover the boxes.

Scissors to cut a small square, at the top of the box, big enough to drop eyeglasses through.

You'll need glue to glue the flyers to the box.

Sample 4—Keeping Track

Organization	Delivered Donation Box	Number of Glasses Collected	Sent Thank-You Note
Mom's work	✓	34	✓
Dad's work	✓	22	✓
School	✓	54	✓
Dr. Elenz's office	✓	31	✓
Dr. Brady's office	✓	47	✓
Dr. Opel's office	✓	28	✓
Dr. Bailey's office	✓	19	✓
Dr. Red's office	✓	51	✓
Dr. Love's office	✓	33	✓
Church's office	✓	109	✓
TOTAL	10 boxes	428	

Sample 5—Thank-You Note

Post a thank-you note at every location of your drop-off boxes. Take a look at the sample letter below.

Dear Dr. Brady, Staff, and Patients,

Thank you for donating your eyeglasses! Without your donation, my eyeglass drive wouldn't have been such a success. I have sent them to an optometrist who volunteers for Unite for Sight. He will be traveling to the rural regions of Africa and China this spring. Your donation will help him succeed with his volunteer work.

Thank you,

Robbie Green

If you want others to be happy, practice compassion. If you want to be happy, practice compassion.—Dalai Lama

Activity 9

Donate Your Hair or Promote Hair Salons to Advertise Hair Donation

If you have long hair and are very brave, this donation drive is for you. This drive is something in which everyone can participate. Growing hair is a natural process, just be sure to keep it healthy.

Step 1

How to begin.

If you have long hair you wish to donate, first find a charity before cutting your hair. Find out what the length requirement is and how they want you to send it. If you want to become a campaign ambassador instead to promote hair donation, find an organization you want to promote and find out how you can advertise at local hair salons. Here are some national nonprofit organizations that make wigs for ill women and children: Locks of Love at www.locksoflove.com or Pantene's Beautiful Lengths at www.beautifullengths.com.

Step 2

Plan a time frame.

If you want to donate your hair and have the length to do it . . . great! If you don't have the length just yet, plan on how long it will take to grow the required length. Take care of it, knowing that one day someone who has lost his or her hair because of illness can benefit from your beautiful locks. Or if you want to promote hair donation, which is just as important as donating your own hair, plan how long you want to campaign. Educate hair salons and hair stylists.

Step 3

Map out where you plan on promoting hair donation.

Make a list of hair salons in your area. Keep track of which salons you have asked to post a poster or flyer. Most salons have booths with individual stylists. Make sure that you speak to not only the manager of the salon but also to each stylist. Ask them if you can post a flyer in their booth or space.

Step 4

How will you be packaging the hair?

A great way to be prepared for packaging hair donation is to request material and information for your promotion and hair donation. You can request the organization to send you 25 hair packaging kits. When I donated 9 inches of my hair, the organization sent me a kit that included a rubber band, a plastic bag, and instructions of the best way to cut and package your lovely locks. This way you can provide salons with packaging kits to give to the hair donors so that they can either package it them- selves or have you pick up the hair donations to send off yourself.

Step 5

Make contact.

Contact the organization. Introduce yourself and explain in full detail why it's important for you to participate in this donation drive. Remember to request 25 hair donation kits. Take notes. See Sample 1.

Step 6

Advertise your promotion for hair donation.

Call your local television station and ask for an interview. Invite them to a beauty shop as you cut your hair or invite the public for a free hairstyle as they donate their hair (with prior permission from the hair salon).

Step 7

Keeping track.

Keep track of the hair salons you have visited. Log how many hair kits they have and how many clients donated the required length of hair. See Sample 2.

Step 8

Send your hair donation!

If you're donating your hair, you should be proud! You've done a great and generous volunteer act. I remember when I donated my hair, it was such a shock to see my hair so short. I had to remind myself that if I felt so different with my hair short, then other people must feel worse when they lose all their hair because of an illness they can't control.

Step 9

Keep a journal.

Did you like campaigning for hair donation? Did you donate your own hair? How did it make you feel?

Step 10

Thank everyone.

Thank the hair salons that have helped you to make the public aware of hair donation. See Sample 3.

Sample 1—Record Keeping

Organization: Beautiful Lengths
Spoke with: Elizabeth Mullen   Date: September 1st
Phone number: 800-000-0012   Contact time: 12:45 p.m.
When will you start your campaign? January 5—May 5
How many hair donation kits will you request? 25
Where will you promote hair donations? At Hair Salons
How will you advertise? I will use the advertising poster and information beautiful lengths supplies on their web site.

Sample 2—Keeping Track

Salon	Manager	Number of Hair Kits	Number of Donors	Thank-You Note Sent
Parkdale Salon	Paula Ames	4	2	✓
Leila's Hair Studio	Jackie Lowe	4	4	✓
Du Wop's Salon	Kevin Spangle	4	3	✓
Freddy & Francesca	Freddy Canales	4	1	✓
Trudy's Salon	Trudy Ingram	4	1	✓
Ocean Drive Salon	Barbara Holland	4	3	✓
Total		24	14	

Sample 3—Thank-You Note

Dear Ocean Drive Salon,

Thank you very much for allowing me to promote hair donation in your salon. I'm so glad that Beautiful Lengths has inspired three of your clients to donate their beautiful hair. Their hair will be made into wigs and will benefit women who have lost their hair because of cancer treatments. Thank you again.

Best,

Brandy Arnold

If you can't feed a hundred people, then feed just one.—Mother Teresa

Activity 10

Nonperishable Food Drive For Families in Need

You can be sure that everyone you ask to help with this drive will participate. This drive would be great right before the holiday season.

Step 1

How to begin.

Find a local or national charity to donate the nonperishable food. Find out what their needs are. Maybe ask for a list of families that are in need. Because cans of food can be too heavy and expensive to mail, I suggest you donate to a local charity. Here are some local organizations found in every city: local community food banks, pantries, and shelters. Take notes. Be sure to document your agenda.

Step 2

Plan a time frame.

When will you plan your perishable food drive? What time of year? How long?

Plan a time frame that works best with your schedule. Also, if you have a list of families who are in need, set a goal of how much nonperishable food you want to raise for each family. Figure out how long it might take to raise these items.

Step 3

Map out where you plan on holding your donation drive.

Will you hold your drive at school? Church? Your parent's workplace? All three places! Make sure that when you do decide on a location, post a list of desired nonperishable food items. Use a very large box to place these goods in. Decorate the box. If it's during the holiday season, use holiday gift wrapping to wrap the box. Post a flyer on the box you've made, expressing what you're asking for, and who you plan on donating the items to.

Step 4

How will you be packaging the items?

Be sure to get sturdy boxes or bins. You can ask a local store if they can give you some of their used boxes. Remember they're free.

Step 5

Make contact.

Contact the organization. Tell them that you are having a nonperishable food drive. Find out how many families are in need. See Sample 1.

Step 6

Advertise your nonperishable food donation drive.

Make flyers or send out e-mail messages. Post your drive in your church newsletter. See Sample 2.

Step 7

Keeping track.

Keep track of where you've placed your box for donations. Check it regularly. Make sure it doesn't overflow with nonperishable food. See Sample 3.

Step 8

Deliver the goods!

Have your mom or dad help you deliver the nonperishable food to the organization. If you can, find out if you can deliver the food to any of the families on your list.

Step 9

Keep a journal.

How do you feel about your nonperishable food drive? Did you enjoy working with your contact organizations? Did you make new friends? Will you have another nonperishable food drive in the near future?

Step 10

Thank everyone.

Post a "Thank-You" flyer at all the donation drive spots.

Remember to remove all the flyers after your event. See Sample 4.

Sample 1—Record Keeping

Charity: Homeless Shelter

Spoke with: Taylor Martin Date: November 5th
Phone number: 784-4063 Contact time: 9:00 a.m.
Do they have pick-up service? No
How will you deliver the donated nonperishable food? Dad will help me.
When will the donation drive begin? November 23—December 23
On what day will the items be delivered to the charity? December 23, 5:30 p.m.
When will you hand out the flyers? November 15
What kinds of items will you request be donated? canned foods and boxed foods

Sample 2—Advertising Flyer

Please Donate Nonperishable Food
Benefiting
The Homeless Shelter
You Can Place Any Canned
or
Nonperishable Boxed Foods
in this box
Items will be picked up weekly beginning
November 23—December 23
Thank you in advance for your donation

Sample 3—Keeping Track

Location	Pickup Date Nov 30	Pickup Date Dec 7	Pickup Date Dec 16	Pickup Date Dec 23
Church	❑	❑	❑	❑
Mom's Workplace	❑	✓	❑	❑
Dad's Workplace	❑	❑	❑	❑
Sun Harvest Grocery Store	❑	❑	❑	❑

Sample 4—Thank-You Note

(To post at your drop-off stations)

Thank you for participating with my annual nonperishable food donation drive.

Your generosity is much appreciated.

Sincerely,

Jon Pettigrove

SECTION TWO

Fund-Raisers

You can't live a perfect day without doing something for someone who will never be able to repay you.—John Wooden

Service to others is the rent you pay for your room here on earth.
—Muhammed Ali

Activity 1

Organize a Garage Sale

This fund-raiser would be great to have during the spring or summer months.

Step 1

How to begin.

Find a local or national charity to donate the funds raised from your garage sale. Get the name of the person with which you made contact. Find out the best way to transfer the funds: check or money order. Also, most organizations allow you to make online donations by going to their web site. Always get your parents' permission before making any online donation. You'll need to have a major credit card in order to process your donation. Be sure to get a receipt for your money donation. Refer to my web site at www.UltimateVolunteer.com for a listing of nonprofit organizations if you need any help deciding which organization you wish to donate to.

Step 2

Plan a time frame.

When will you plan your garage sale? Be sure not to pick a holiday weekend like Labor Day or Columbus Day. Families usually plan a long holiday weekend on those days. Also, if you're familiar with the typical forecast in your area, plan a weekend or Saturday on a nice sunny day. Don't forget the complimentary lemonade!

Step 3

Location.

The great thing about holding your fund-raiser in your garage is that if it starts to rain your items will be safe from getting wet. You can possibly ask your neighbors to have a garage sale on the same day you have your fund-

raising garage sale. They don't have to use their proceeds toward a charity, but sometimes people like to shop at many garage sales in one location.

Step 4

How will you manage the money raised from your fund-raiser?

Where will you keep your money? Will you keep a log book for every cent
that goes into it? I suggest keeping a money box. Also, be sure to have
upfront money for your garage sale. You can't start your garage sale without any change.

Step 5

Make contact.

Make contact with the organization to which you plan on donating your
money. Tell them how you plan on raising the money. Tell them why you
chose their organization. See Sample 1.

Step 6

Advertise your garage sale.

Contact your local newspaper and advertise it there. Make signs and post
them at the end of your block. Remember to remove all the flyers after
your event. See Samples 2 and 3.

Step 7

Keep track.

As you sell items from your garage sale, keep a log book of what you sold
and for how much. See Sample 4.

Step 8

Keep a journal.

Did you enjoy having your fund-raising garage sale? Did you expect to
raise as much money? Journal your experience with your fund-raiser.

Step 9

Send the money!

If you send the money by check, be sure to double-check the mailing
address. You can also donate online. You'll have to use your mom or dad's

credit card or bank card to donate funds online. If you donate this way, be sure to give the money to your mom or dad to make the payment back to the credit card or deposit the money back into their bank account.

Step 10

Thank everyone.

Thank your parents for helping you with your garage sale. Thank the people who purchased items from your garage sale as they leave.

Sample 1—Record Keeping

Charity: Save the Children Federation, Inc.
Spoke with: Rosie Cantrell Date: July 2nd
Phone number: 800-728-3843   Contact time: 3:30 p.m.
Web site: www.charitablechoiccs.org
Mailing address: 54 Wilton Rd., Westport, CT 06886
How will you donate the money? Cashiers Check
Why did you choose this charity? Because I'm a kid too and I want to help other kids.
When are you having your garage sale? Saturday, July 12
Where are you having your garage sale? At my house

Sample 2—Advertisement Sign

Fund-raising
Garage Sale
612 Garden St.
Today
Saturday, July 12th
7:00—10 a.m.

Sample 3—Newspaper Ad

Fund-raising Garage Sale, 612 Garden Street, Saturday, July 12th, 7:00-10 a.m.

Sample 4—Keeping Track

Item	Sold For
Flower pot	.50

Plaid men's shirt	$1.00
Bag of magnets	.25
Roller Skates	$2.00
Fishing cap	.75
Bedskirt	$3.25
Box of baseball cards	$5.00
Tamborine	$1.25
Skirt	$1.00
Vest	.75
Microwave	$15.00
Blanket	$2.00
Old chair	$20.00
Sneakers	$1.00
Fishing pole	$6.00
Total	$59.75

We cannot always build the future for our youth, but we can build our youth for the future.—Franklin Delano Roosevelt

Activity 2

Penny Drive at Your School

Raise Funds for an Organization of Your Choice

This is a fun drive for kids! Everyone has pennies they can donate.

Step 1

Make contact.

Find a local or national charity to donate the funds raised from your penny drive. Get the name of the person with which you made contact with. Tell that person how you plan on raising the money. Tell that person why you chose his or her organization. Find out what the best way to transfer the funds: check or money order. Also, most organizations allow you to make online donations by going to their web site. Always get your parents' permission before making any online donation. You'll need to have a major credit card in order to process your donation. Be sure to get a receipt for your money donation. Refer to www.UltimateVolunteer.com for a listing of nonprofit organizations if you need any help deciding which organization you wish to donate to. See Sample 1.

Step 2

Plan a time frame.

How long do you expect to hold your penny fund-raiser? One week, two weeks, three weeks? Make sure you plan well. This type of fund-raiser can be so much fun that you forget how long it's been since you started it! Remember to get the penny rollers from the bank well in advance.

Step 3

Find a location.

Before you start your penny drive at school, be sure to get permission from your school principal. Then, you'll need to plan on how you will collect pennies from all your fellow students. I suggest getting empty 5 gallon water bottles, used for water dispensers, and labeling each one with a number representing each grade level at your school. You can have a challenge between grade levels. It will make for good fun and excitement with a great visual display.

Step 4

How will you manage the money raised from your fund-raiser?

For your penny drive, you might want to have your friends or family help you count the pennies to put them in the penny rollers. When I was a kid, I used to love looking at the year each penny was made. Fun games can make the task less tedious.

Step 5

Supply list.

Make a list of all the items you will need for your penny drive. See Sample 2.

Step 6

Advertise your penny drive.

Make a morning announcement at school. Tell your classmates to participate with your penny drive. See Sample 3.

Step 7

Keeping track.

One good way to keep track of how your penny drive is going is to put percentage markers on each empty 5 gallon water bottle. Each marker represents approximately how much a grade level has contributed. See Sample 4.

Step 8

Keep a journal.

Did you have fun with your penny drive? Did any of your friends help you with your penny drive? Write down all your thoughts and feelings of your event.

Step 9

Send the money!

Don't send the penny rollers. Change them with a local bank. If the organization wants a money order, ask the bank for a money order.

Step 10

Thank everyone.

Thank all your classmates for their help with your penny drive. Post a thank-you flyer at school or thank them during your school's morning announcements. See Sample 5.

Sample 1—Record Keeping

Charity: Parkinson's Disease Foundation

Spoke with: Glenn Allen   Date: March 4th
Phone number: 800-457-6676   Contact time: 4:00 p.m.
Web site: www.parkinson.org
Mailing address: 1501 NW 9th Ave., Bob Hope Road, Miami, FL 33136
How will you donate the money? Send a check by mail
Why is it important to you to donate to this charity? Because Aunt Beth suffers from this disease.

Sample 2—Supply List

Table
6 empty 5-gallon water bottles
black paper
letter & number templates
glue

Sample 3—Announcement at School

Attention Classmates!
I'd like to announce that we are having a class penny war beginning on Monday, September 25th for one week.
We will have water bottles set up on a table in the foyer representing each grade level. The donated pennies will go to the Parkinson's Disease Foundation. Please participate in this charitable and fun event. The class winner will receive bragging rights for the rest of the school year!

Sample 4—Keeping Track

	1st Week	2nd Week	3rd Week	4th Week	Total
Kindergarten	5%	10%	20%	35%	
1st Grade	15%	25%	35%	50%	
2nd Grade	10%	20%	25%	40%	
3rd Grade	15%	20%	30%	60%	3rd Grade!
4th Grade	20%	30%	35%	50%	
5th Grade	5%	15%	20%	30%	

Your table can be displayed like this:

100%	100%	100%	100%	100%	100%
90%	90%	90%	90%	90%	90%
80%	80%	80%	80%	80%	80%
70%	70%	70%	70%	70%	70%
60%	60%	60%	60%	60%	60%
50%	50%	50%	50%	50%	50%
40%	40%	40%	40%	40%	40%
30%	30%	30%	30%	30%	30%
20%	20%	20%	20%	20%	20%
10%	10%	10%	10%	10%	10%
K	1st	2nd	3rd	4th	5th

WINNER has bragging rights for the remainder of the school year.

Sample 5—Thank-You Announcement

Good morning fellow classmates!

I'd like to announce the winner of this year's penny war . . . however I'd like to first thank everyone for participating in this event, everyone who contributed helped a great deal to raise $724.37 for the Parkinson's Disease Foundation . . . so thank you very much.

All right, now for this year's penny war class winner . . . and the winner is Third Grade!

Congratulations you have bragging rights, this year, as the penny war class champions.

Have a great day!

Volunteers don't get paid, not because they're worthless,
but because they're priceless.—Author Unknown

Activity 3

Bake Sale with Your Friends and Use the Proceeds Toward a Charity

Yummy . . . Yummy . . . this fund-raiser is sure to be a hit for everyone! It can be conducted anytime of year. Just try not to eat all your delicious goods.

Step 1

How to begin.

Find a local or national charity to donate the funds raised from your bake sale. Get the name of the person with which you made contact. Find out the best way to transfer the funds: check or money order. Also, most organizations allow you to make online donations by going to their web site. Always get your parents' permission before making any online donation. You'll need to have a major credit card in order to process your donation. Be sure to get a receipt for your money donation. Refer to my web site at www.UltimateVolunteer.com for a listing of nonprofit organizations if you need any help deciding which organization you wish to donate to.

Step 2

Plan a time frame.

How long will you have your bake sale? On what day, week, or weekend? Invite your friends to participate in this fund-raiser. Ask them to bake their favorite dessert. To add on to your sales potential, you could sell the recipe card for each treat. Have everyone, including yourself, make recipe cards of each dessert. You can bet that your delicious desserts will taste great, and everyone will want to know how you made it. This is a great way to raise more money for your charity.

Step 3

Map out where you plan on holding your bake sale.

Where will you have your bake sale? Will you sell your desserts outside a grocery store? At a local post office? At a local theater during intermission? My hometown has a local used bookshop where you can purchase coffee and cappuccinos, but they don't sell pastries. Maybe you have a similar bookstore? Perhaps you could sell your treats at a local soccer game, baseball game, football game, or basketball game. You might even run out of your desserts at one of these events!

Step 4

How will you be packaging the items?

To have a beautiful and appealing display, I recommend using a nice tablecloth to place under your baked goods. Have at least one cake-covered dish displayed in the middle of your table. You'll need small plastic or paper plates and plastic forks to serve cake. If you're making cookies or cupcakes, you won't need the forks or plates, but you'll need to pass out napkins with the treats. Remember to always use plastic gloves if the dessert is not wrapped with plastic wrap.

Step 5

Make contact.

Contact the organization to which you plan on donating your money. Tell them how you will raise money for their organization. Let them know why their organization is important to you. See Sample 1.

Step 6

Baking planner.

Write down what kinds of desserts you plan on baking. If you're asking your friends to help with your fund-raiser, ask them what they plan on baking. Plan ahead by making a grocery list of the ingredients needed. See Sample 2.

Step 7

Advertise your bake sale.

Whether you plan on having your bake sale at a game or a local coffee shop you will need to advertise why you're there. Be sure to have a flyer posted at your table stand with the oranization's name and Web site that you're raising money for. Fans love to munch on goodies while they're watching any sporting event and people love to eat treats with their cappuccinos. Just be sure to get permission from the manager of the store or local sporting event organization. See Sample 3.

Step 8

Keep track.

Keep track of which desserts sold well. For future reference, this information is important to remember. List how many cookies were sold. How many cupcakes? This kind of information should be written in your volunteer journal. See Sample 4.

Step 9

Send the money!

How will you send the money? By check or money order? Will you make an online donation? Make it easy for you and your family. Also, make sure you have the right mailing address.

Step 10

Thank everyone.

Thank your mom or dad for helping you with the baking and setting up. If your friends helped you, thank them for making your bake sale a successful event. Also thank people as they purchase your pastries. See Sample 5.

Sample 1—Record Keeping

Charity: Honduras Hope

Spoke with: Valerie Trejo   Date: April 3rd
Phone number: 603-823-5262   Contact time: 10:00 a.m.
Web site: www.hondurashope.org
How will you donate the money? An online donation
Why is it important to you to donate to this charity? Because my family is originally from Honduras.
Where will you have your bake sale? At the baseball tournament, the weekend of April 23rd and 24th
Who will be helping you with your bake sale? My friends: Henry, Mary, Sarah, Tiffany, J. K., William, and Courtney

Sample 2—Baking Planner

Who's Baking What?

	Choco Cake	Sugar Cook.	Cup Cake	Recipe Cards	Nut Bread	Peanut Brittle	Brown-ies	Choco Chip
Me	✓			✓				
Henry			✓	✓				
Mary		✓		✓				
Sarah				✓	✓			
Tiffany				✓				✓
J.K.				✓			✓	
William				✓				
Courtney				✓		✓		

Sample 3—Advertisement Flyers

Bake Sale
All Proceeds Donated to Honduras Hope
www.hondurashope.org

Sample 4—Keeping Track

	How Many Made	How Many Sold	$ Amount Earned
Chocolate cake	2	16 slices	$16.00
Sugar cookies	48	48	$12.00
Cupcakes	48	48	$24.00
Recipe cards	12 each	66	$16.50
Brownies	24	19	$9.50
Chocolate chip cookies	48	43	$10.75
Banana nut bread	24 slices	15 slices	$15.00
Peanut brittle	48	46	$23.00
Total			$173.25

Sample 5—Thank-You Notes

Thank-you note to parents:
Mom and Dad,
Thank you for helping me with the bake sale. Without your help it wouldn't

have been a success.
I love you,
Beth

Thank-you note to your friends:
William,
Thank you for baking chocolate chip cookies for the bake sale. Without your help and support, we wouldn't have raised as much money as we did for Honduras Hope. You are truly a good friend.
Your Friend,
Beth

Unless someone like you cares a whole awful lot, nothing is
going to get better. It's not.—Dr. Seuss

Activity 4

Auction Chores and Use the Proceeds toward a Charity

This fund-raiser requires adult supervision at all time. Be sure to be thorough with your chores.

Step 1

Make contact.

Find a local or national charity to donate the funds raised from your auction. Contact the organization of choice. Get the name of the person with which you made contact. Tell that person why it's important for you to raise money for his or her organization. Don't forget to write down their address. Take notes. Find out the best way to transfer the funds: check or money order. Also, most organizations allow you to make online donations by going to their web site. Always get your parents' permission before making any online donation. You'll need to have a major credit card in order to process your donation. Be sure to get a receipt for your money donation. Refer to my web site at www.UltimateVolunteer.com for a listing of nonprofit organizations if you need any help deciding which organization you wish to donate to. See Sample 1.

Step 2

Plan a time frame.

When do you plan on auctioning off chores to your neighbors or family? Ask your friends to participate with this fund-raiser. Be sure to designate one week, two weeks, or even three weeks to have your calendar ready of your schedule for your fund-raiser. One good way to do this is when you auction off your chores have your calendar ready to schedule your chore date and time with the person who is buying it. This way, you know ahead of time what work you have to do.

Step 3

How will you contact others to buy your chores?

How will you auction off your chores? Will you make phone calls or go door to door to ask your family and neighbors if you could cut their grass, water their plants, sweep their sidewalk, etc.? Make a list of chores you can do and would like to do. See Sample 2.

Step 4

Advertise your auction.

When you advertise your auction, do not limit yourself to simply dusting or cutting grass. Advertise that you are willing to wash cars or rake leaves. Show them your list of chores that you are willing to do. Also, remember not to commit yourself to a chore that could be too dangerous. Your parents should approve the list of chores you will be auctioning to ensure your safety. Remember to always have one of your parents present during your chore activity. See Sample 3.

Step 5

Auction cards.

Make and hand out auction cards. Make a handful of cards for the same chore with different dollar amounts on each card. The person buying the chore can either choose to pay the most dollar amount for the chore or the least dollar amount for the chore. See Sample 4.

Step 6

Keep track.

Keep track of all your clients. It's very important to be on time to each and every appointment. Keep in mind that you're working very hard for a great cause. Good for you! See Sample 5.

Step 7

Supply list.

Be prepared to have the supplies needed for your auctioned-off chores. Take a look at your appointments. Write down what you'll need. See Sample 6.

Step 8

Keep a journal.

Did you enjoy this fund-raiser? Write down all your experiences in your journal.

Step 9

Send the money off!

Find out the best way to send your money. By check or money order? Never send cash, it is impossible to track. You can also send your payment online to many organizations. Most nonprofit organizations have a payment section on their web site. Ask your contact person if this is the best way to send your generous donation.

Step 10

Thank everyone.

Send a thank-you note to all the people who participated with your auction. See Sample 7.

Sample 1—Record Keeping

Charity: Prevent Child Abuse America

Spoke with: Benjamin Scott   Date: August 8th
Phone number: 1-800-CHILDREN   Contact time: 1:30 p.m.
Web site: www.preventchildabuse.org
Mailing address: Prevent Child Abuse America, 500 N. Michigan Avenue, Suite 200, Chicago, IL 60611
How will you donate the money? Check by mail
Why is it important to you to donate to this charity? This charity is important to me because I want to help with the prevention and awareness of child abuse.
Who will you ask to buy your chores? Neighbors, Family, Friends, and Relatives
How will you contact your family and neighbors? I'll call my family and go door to door in my neighborhood.

Sample 2—List of chores I can do

Wash cars
Clean windows
Mow lawns
Rake leaves
Sweep driveways and sidewalks
Trim shrubs
Water grass

Iron clothes
Clean a garage
Take out trash
Paint a fence
Vacuum carpet
Water plants
Dust
Organize an area

Sample 3—Advertisement Flyer

Chores Auction Benefiting
Prevent Child Abuse America www.preventchildabuse.org
Here's how it works:
Please select an Auction Chore Card and Schedule an Appointment.
Each chore card has a dollar amount listed. You can pay me after I have
completed the chore.
Thank you in advance for your time and hopefully a needed chore.
Sincerely,
Johan Greer

Sample 4—Sample Auction Chore Cards

Auction Card	Auction Card	Auction Card	Auction Card	Auction Card	Auction Card
Wash Cars $15.00	Wash Cars $12.00	Wash Cars $10.00	Wash Cars $8.00	Wash Cars $5.00	Wash Cars $4.00
Auction Card	Auction Card	Auction Card	Auction Card	Auction Card	Auction Card
Clean Windows $15.00	Clean Windows $12.00	Clean Windows $10.00	Clean Windows $8.00	Clean Windows $5.00	Clean Windows $4.00
Auction Card	Auction Card	Auction Card	Auction Card	Auction Card	Auction Card
Mow Lawn $ 15.00	Mow Lawn $ 10.00	Mow Lawn $10.00	Mow Lawn $8.00	Mow Lawn $5.00	Mow Lawn $4.00
Auction Card	Auction Card	Auction Card	Auction Card	Auction Card	Auction Card
Rake Leaves $15.00	Rake Leaves $10.00	Rake Leaves $10.00	Rake Leaves $8.00	Rake Leaves $5.00	Rake Leaves $4.00
Auction Card	Auction Card	Auction Card	Auction Card	Auction Card	Auction Card
Paint Fence $50.00	Paint Fence $45.00	Paint Fence $42.00	Paint Fence $40.00	Paint Fence $38.00	Paint Fence $35.00

Sample 5—Keeping Track/Appointment Log

	Mon	Tues	Wed	Thurs	Fri	Sat
8 a.m.		Paint fence		Clean		Mow lawn
		Ken Newly		Garage		Quinn
		$50.00		Luke Gary		Pettigrove
				$35.00		$15.00
9 a.m.	Trim	Paint fence	Clean	Clean		Mow lawn
	Shrubs	Ken Newly	Windows	Garage		Quinn
	Lynette Jobe		Laura Rose	Luke Gary		Pettigrove
	$10.00		$12.00			
10 a.m.		Paint fence		Clean		Mow lawn
		Ken Newly		Garage		Quinn
				Luke Gary		Pettigrove
11 a.m.		Paint fence		Clean		Mow lawn
		Ken Newly		Garage		Quinn
				Luke Gary		Pettigrove
12 p.m.	Lunch	Lunch	Lunch	Lunch	Lunch	Lunch
1 p.m.	Wash Cars	Paint fence	Iron		Rake	
	Mae Tully	Ken Newly	Clothes		Leaves	
	$12.00		Holly Hall		Kelly Undra	
			$10.00		$8.00	
2 p.m.	Wash Cars	Paint fence	Iron		Rake	
	Mae Tully	Ken Newly	Clothes		Leaves	
			Holly Hall		Kelly Undra	
3 p.m.	Wash Cars	Paint fence	Iron		Rake	
	Mae Tully	Ken Newly	Clothes		Leaves	
			Holly Hall		Kelly Undra	
4 p.m.		Paint fence	Iron		Rake	
		Ken Newly	Clothes		Leaves	
			Holly Hall		Kelly Undra	
5 p.m.		Paint fence				
		Ken Newly				
	$22.00	$50.00	$22.00	$35.00	$8.00	$15.00

Total Weekly Earnings: $152.00

Sample 6—Supply List

Large sponge—To use when you're washing cars
Bucket
Car soap—To use when you're washing cars
Hedge clippers
Leather gloves- to protect your hands from blistering
Eye goggles
Glass cleaner
12 x 12 pieces of cotton cloth (for dusting and drying cars)
Lawn mower
Rake
Lawn bags
Paint brush
Iron
Starch—To use while you're ironing clothes
Broom

Sample 7—Thank-You Note

Dear Mrs. Perry,
Thank you for hiring me to mow your lawn. I hope I did a good job. Also, thank you for helping me raise money for Prevent Child Abuse America. The $15.00 dollars you paid me will go toward this charity.
Your neighbor,

Johan Greer

Volunteers do not necessarily have the time; they just have the heart.
—Elizabeth Andrew, Humanitarian

Activity 5

Auction Donated Items and Use the Proceeds Toward a Charity

This fund-raiser requires a lot of creative thinking. Use your best skills to think of items on which people might want to bid.

Step 1

How to begin.

Find a local or national charity to donate the funds raised from your auction. Get the name of the person with which you made contact. Find out the best way to transfer the funds: check or money order. Also, most organizations allow you to make online donations by going to their web site. Always get your parents' permission before making any online donation. You'll need to have a major credit card in order to process your donation. Be sure to get a receipt for your money donation. Refer to my web site at www.UltimateVolunteer.com for a list of nonprofit organizations if you need any help deciding which organization you wish to donate to. Take notes. See Sample 1.

Step 2

Plan a time frame.

When will you plan your auction? How long will you hold your auction? Will you make it a casual event, a semiformal event, or black-tie event? Will you use a social event already planned to auction off your items? Be sure to plan well and make it fun!

Step 3

Map out where you plan on holding your auction.

Where will you have your auction? One great place that comes to mind is at a bingo hall. Usually at a bingo hall, someone is on the microphone calling out letters and numbers. This is a great opportunity to ask the manager if you could auction off your donated items for your charity while using their audience and equipment.

Step 4

How will you be packaging the items?

When you plan your auction, you need to think about how you will present each item. For example, if you have a local movie theater donate two tickets, a large-size popcorn and a large coke, how will you package the coupons or tickets? Maybe you could ask the movie theater to give you a small popcorn box, and you could fill the bottom with glittery stuffing and place the tickets and coupons at top. Be creative!

Step 5

Make description cards.

Before your auction, write a brief description of each item. This will help you present the items in a good way and you won't forget how. Also, remember to mention the business who donated the item or items. See Sample 2.

Step 6

Advertise your auction.

Make a flyer and be sure to advertise two weeks before your auction. Post your flyer around the location where you've planned your auction. Invite your family and friends to the location of your auction. See Sample 3.

Step 7

Keep track.

Keep track of who donated the items for your auction. List the items and their value. Also, keep track of their final auction price. See Sample 4.

Step 8

Keep a journal.

Was your auction fun? Did you make any friends? Write your experiences and thoughts about your auction.

Step 9

Send the money!

How will you send your money? Will you make an online payment or send a money order? All nonprofit organizations have a web site with a link to make a monetary contribution. Discuss this with your mom or dad. Do what's best for you, and make it an easy transaction.

Step 10

Thank everyone.

Thank the people who purchased each item by attaching thank-you notes. Have generic thank-you notes attached to each item. See Sample 5. Be sure not to forget to thank the business or organization that let you use their space for your auction, and who donated items for your auction. See Sample 5.

Sample 1—Record Keeping

Charity: Ronald McDonald House

Spoke with: Benjamin Scott   Date: August 8th
Phone number: 630-623-7048   Contact time: 1:30 p.m.
Web site: www.rmhc.com
Mailing address: Ronald McDonald House Charities, One Kroc Drive, Oak Brook, IL 60523
How will you donate the money? Check by mail
Why is it important to you to donate to this charity? Because there are so many families that are in need of the Ronald McDonald House, and I want to help those families.
Who will you ask to buy your chores? Neighbors, Family, Friends, Relatives
Where will you have your auction? At the bingo hall
Spoke to: Fred Adamson   Date: February 11th
Phone number: 222-847-2200   Contact time: 5:00 p.m.
Who will make the announcement? My dad who has experience
What time will the auction start? 8 p.m.

Sample 2—Donated Item Write-Up

Item: Two movie tickets, large popcorn, (2) large drinks, (2) candies
Alright folks, first up we have a great movie package donated from Cinema House. It includes two movie tickets to view any movie playing at Cinema House, one large buttery warm popcorn, two large cold refreshing drinks,

and any two candy bars of your choice. This package is valued at $55.00. The movie tickets are for any movie and for any showing of any day. This lovely movie package does not have an expiration date. Ok, lets start the bidding. . . . We're starting these items at $12.00. . . . Do I have a bidder at $12.00.

Sample 3—Advertisement Flyer

Don't Miss the Auction
Tuesday, February 11th at 8:00 p.m.
There will be many items to bid on!
Proceeds will benefit the Ronald McDonald House
www.rmhc.com

Sample 4—Keeping Track

Donated Items from Organizations:

Donor	Donation	Value	Sent Thank -You
Bath and Body Works	Gift basket	$50.00	✓
Cinema House	2 tickets and refreshments	$55.00	✓
Sunrise Mall	General Gift certificate	$50.00	✓
Jiffy Lube	Free oil change	$25.00	✓
Barnes & Noble	Gift Certificate	$25.00	✓
Tom's Video Store	Coupon for 10 free rentals	$30.00	✓
Laguna Tan	10 Free tanning sessions	$50.00	✓
Seaside Golf	1 Free 18 hole golf game	$25.00	✓
Sam's Club	1 month of membership	$15.00	✓
Trudy's Beauty Salon	Haircut and style	$60.00	✓

Donor	Value	Auction off
Bath and Body Works	$50.00	$35.00
Cinema House	$45.00	$20.00
Sunrise Mall	$50.00	$25.00
Jiffy Lube	$25.00	$10.00
Barnes & Noble	$25.00	$10.00
Tom's Video Store	$30.00	$13.00

Laguna Tan $50.00 $20.00
Seaside Golf $25.00 $10.00
Sam's Club $15.00 $5.00
Trudy's Beauty Salon $60.00 $30.00
Total Earned: $178.00

Sample 5—Thank-you Note

Thank the bingo hall for letting you use their business to hold your auction.

Mr. Adamson,

Thank you very much for letting me use your bingo hall for my auction. If it weren't for you, my auction wouldn't have been such a success.

Sam Elliott

Thank the companies who donated their products.

Mrs. Cortez,

Thank you so much for donating a lovely basket full of Bath and Body Works products. Without your help and donation, my auction wouldn't have been successful.

Sam Elliot

Scratch a dog and you'll find a permanent job.
—Franklin P. Jones, Businessman

Activity 6

Bathe Dogs from your Neighborhood or Local Area for a Donation and use Proceeds toward your Favorite Charity

This fund-raiser should be conducted during the spring or summer, and your mom or dad should always be present to help you. Have fun!

Step 1

Find a charity.

Find a local or national charity to donate the funds raised from bathing the dogs. Get the name of the person with which you made contact. Find out the best way to transfer the funds: check or money order. Also, most organizations allow you to make online donations by going to their web site. Always get your parents' permission before making any online donation. You'll need to have a major credit card in order to process your donation. Be sure to get a receipt for your money donation. Refer to my web site at www.UltimateVolunteer.com for a list of nonprofit organizations if you need any help deciding which organization you wish to donate to. Take notes.

Step 2

Make contact.

After choosing your nonprofit organization, contact the director. Tell him or her how you are raising money for his or her organization. Express why donating money to this organization is important to you. Explain how you are going to do it and ask for suggestions. See Sample 1.

Step 3

Plan a time frame.

When do you plan on bathing dogs for a money donation? What time of year? What week or weekend? How long? Get some tips from a local veterinarian on how to bathe dogs. Also, be sure to use shampoo that's recommended for dogs only. Maybe ask a local pet store to donate dog shampoo . . . remember it doesn't hurt to ask.

Step 4

Map out where you plan on holding your fund-raiser.

Where will you bathe the dogs? A dog park? Will you bathe the dog in the front yard of the dog owner's home? If you do this you need to make sure you always have an adult present. Also, you will need to ask if you could use their water hose.

Step 5

Leave your mark.

After each dog you bathe, leave something creative with them. Give their owner a dog bone with a ribbon wrapped around it and a tag that reads "thank you." Be creative and give them a great memory!

Step 6

Advertise your fund-raiser.

Ask local veterinarian offices to post flyers of your event. Also, put your flyers in your neighbor's mailboxes. See Sample 2.

Step 7

Keep track.

Keep track of how many dogs you bathed. Did you meet your goal? See Sample 3.

Step 8

Keep a journal.

Did you have fun! Did you enjoy bathing dogs? Write down all your experiences with your fund-raiser.

Step 9

Send the money off!

Never send cash through the mail. Send a check or money order only. You could also make a money donation by going to the organization's web site. There, you should always find a "donate now" link.

Step 10

Thank everyone.

Remember to say "Thank You" when you've finished bathing each dog. Give the dog a dog biscuit. Be sure each customer knows where the money is headed and who it will benefit.

Sample 1—Record Keeping

Charity: The Humane Society of the United States

Spoke with: Heidi Walker   Date: August 30th
Phone number: 202-452-1100   Contact time: 1:00 p.m.
Web site: www.hsus.org
How will you donate the money? Online Donation
Why is it important to you to donate to this charity? I love animals! I want to help all the animals in the world.
Who will you ask to buy your chores? Neighbors, Family, Friends, and Relatives
What kinds of products do you need? Dog Shampoo, Dog Shampoo for Sensitive Skin, Bucket, Dog Brush, Dog Treats.
Will anyone help you? Yes, my friends Becky and June . . . and my mom.

Sample 2—Advertisement Flyer

Is your dog smelly?
If your answer is "yes," I can fix your problem!
I am hosting a dog bathing rally Benefiting The Humane Society of America
www.hsus.org
All proceeds will go to this charity!
Saturday, September 6th at Lamar Park from 9 a.m.–3 p.m.

Sample 3—Keeping Track

Owner	Dog's Name	Dog Breed	Any Skin Allergies	Amount Earned
Kim Soliz	Mimi	Poodle		$10.00
Doug Savage	Pookie	Dalmatian	Yes	$10.00
Sara Reynolds	Dingo	Bull Dog		$10.00

Orlando Little	Gizmo	Terrier mix		$10.00
La Rhonda Williams	Jazz	Cocker Spaniel		$10.00
Freddy Ortiz	Taco	Chihuahua		$5.00
Lisa Holland	Princess	Chow mix		$10.00
Betsy Harris	Winnie	Golden Retriever		$10.00
Kite Warren	Buck	Bird Dog mix		$10.00
Jimmy Blaine	Jack	Jack Russell	Yes	$10.00
Molly Garland	Nicky	Spaniel mix		$10.00
LaVera Long	Bingo	Lab mix		$10.00
Parker McKenzie	Jingle	King Charles Spaniel		$10.00
Rich Mazzie	Harper	St. Bernard		$10.00
Total:				$140.00

*I will be riding a bike in 10 years time because I feel better when I do
exercise and I want to enjoy true good health.—Lance Armstrong*

Activity 7

Conduct a Walk-A-Thon

Walk, Run, or Bike a Half-A-Marathon

A half-a-marathon is approximately 13 miles. Ask people to give you $1
for every mile achieved. Be sure to drink plenty of water and wear protective sun block. Good luck!

Step 1

Make contact.

Find a local or national charity to donate the funds raised from your half-
a-marathon. Contact the nonprofit organization that you've selected. Tell
them about your half-a-marathon. Express why you chose their organization. Find out which is the best way to transfer the funds: check or money
order. Also, most organizations allow you to make online donations by
going to their web site. Always get your parents' permission before making any online donation. You'll need to have a major credit card in order
to process your donation. Be sure to get a receipt for your money donation. Refer to my web site at www.UltimateVolunteer.com for a list of nonprofit organizations if you need any help deciding which organization you
wish to donate to. See Sample 1.

Step 2

Plan a time frame.

When will you walk, run, or bike your half-a-marathon? What day? What
time of year? Whichever time of year you decide, be prepared to wear the
proper protective gear. Also, you can try to obtain a sponsor to advertise
your event. Ask local bicycle shops or sports shops to sponsor you. Have
your mom or dad participate in this event. You can have them drive their
car behind you just like the professionals do. You'll need parent supervision with this event!

Step 3

Map out where you plan on holding your half-a-marathon.

Where will you conduct your half-a-marathon? At a local track? At a local park? Wherever you decide, make sure you and your parents count the exact amount of miles.

Step 4

Exercise.

Before your big day you'll need to build up your endurance by exercising everyday. Keep a log of the miles that you've completed on a daily basis. Give yourself a few months of training. See Sample 2.

Step 5

Eat well.

As you're training, plan a nutritious eating plan. Remember to eat a balanced meal and take your daily vitamin.

Step 6

Advertise.

Call your local newspaper before your event. Call your local news station and invite an anchorperson to the finish line.

Step 7

Send out invitations.

Send invitations to your family and friends. Don't forget to invite your sponsors. See Sample 3.

Step 8

Keeping track.

Make a list of the people who donated to every mile. See Sample 4.

Step 9

Send the money!

Send your check or money order. Do not send cash. Also, you can make your contribution at the organization's web site. Do what's easiest for you.

Step 10

Thank everyone.

Send thank-you notes to everyone who contributed. Tell your parents how much they mean to you and that you couldn't have done it without them. See Sample 5.

Sample 1—Record Keeping

Charity: Breast Cancer Fund

Spoke with: Megan Dietz, Office Assistance   Date: March 27th
Phone number: 415-346-8223   Contact time: 2:30 p.m.
Web site: www.breastcancerfund.org
E-mail: Megan.Dietz@BreastCancerfund.com
Mailing address: 1388 Sutter Street Suite 400, San Francisco, CA 84109
How will you send the money? I will send a money order.
Where are you conducting your half-a-marathon? The half-a-marathon will be conducted at the Webster High School track.
What date will you conduct your half-a-marathon? Saturday, April 21st.
How many miles are you planning on achieving? 13

Sample 2—Walking Log Book

Date	Miles	Time to walk, run, or bike the mile(s)
February 3	2 miles	28 minutes (Beginning date)
February 4	2 miles	29 minutes
February 5	2.5 miles	35 minutes
February 6	1.5 miles	21 minutes
February 7	2.5 miles	34 minutes
February 8	3 miles	43 minutes
February 9	3 miles	42 minutes
February 10	3.5 miles	50 minutes
February 11	3.5 miles	52 minutes
February 12	4 miles	60 minutes
February 13	4 miles	58 minutes
February 14	3.5 miles	50 minutes
February 15	3.5 miles	49 minutes
February 16	4 miles	60 minutes
February 17	4.5 miles	63 minutes

February 18	4.5 miles	64 minutes
February 19	3.5 miles	47 minutes
February 20	3 miles	40 minutes
February 21	3.5 miles	45 minutes
February 22	4 miles	58 minutes
February 23	4.5 miles	60 minutes
February 24	4.5 miles	58 minutes
February 25	3 miles	40 minutes
February 26	3 miles	40 minutes
February 27	3.5 miles	44 minutes

Sample 3—Invitation

You're Invited to Martin's Half-a-Marathon
on Saturday, April 21st at 9 a.m.
Webster High School's Track and Field

Sample 4—Keeping Track

Contributors	Donated	Sent Thank-You Notes
Linda Farmer	$13.00	❏
Hope Farrell	$13.00	❏
Arnold Lopez	$13.00	❏
Vivian Hill	$13.00	❏
Bob Cox	$13.00	❏
Rob and Renee Davis	$13.00	❏
Angie Dillon	$13.00	❏
Courtney Robins	$13.00	❏
Maxwell Carter	$13.00	❏
Rowan Newton	$13.00	❏

Sample 5—Thank-You Note

Dear Hope Farrell,

Thank you very much for donating $1.00 for each mile I walked. Your contribution will go toward the Breast Cancer Fund that helps fund education and advocacy programs to fight the elimination of breast cancer.

Thank you,

Martin Grey

I am thankful for the mess to clean after a party because it means I have been surrounded by friends.—Nancie J. Carmody, Author

Activity 8

Host A Murder Mystery Party

Sell Seats for Your Party; Use all Proceeds toward a Charity

This fund-raiser is super fun! This fund-raiser requires significant party planning. Your guests are sure to have a blast.

Step 1

Make contact.

Find a local or national charity to donate the funds raised from your murder mystery party. Contact the nonprofit organization that you've selected. Tell them about your murder mystery party. Express why you chose their organization.

Get the name of the person with whom you made contact. Find out the best way to transfer the funds: check, money order. Most organizations allow you to make online donations by going to their web site. Always get your parents' permission before making any online donation. You'll need to have a major credit card in order to process your donation.

Be sure to get a receipt for your money donation. Refer to my web site at www.UltimateVolunteer.com for a list of nonprofit organizations if you need any help deciding which organization you wish to donate to. See Sample 1.

Step 2

Plan a time frame.

What day will you host your murder mystery party? What time? How much will you ask each guest to donate? Make sure you schedule it early enough to end before normal bedtime hours. When I've hosted a murder mystery party, it always took at least four hours from start to finish. You can go online to order a murder mystery game. It costs approximately $15–$25. Or you can buy a used game that can cost less. The games usually come with a host on a CD that takes you through the game. The game always comes with a theme, invitations, and a recommended menu. It also has the option of how many guests you can invite. Not all games have the option of having ten or more players. Search for the company-size murder mystery games if you plan on selling 15 or more seats. Or if you're familiar with murder mystery games, you can write your own script.

Step 3

Where will you have your murder mystery party?

Do you have enough space at your home? You can always check to see if a local hall can donate their space for one afternoon to host your murder mystery party. Choose a game that suggests easy foods to make so that you won't need a kitchen.

Step 4

Supply list.

Make a list of supplies you'll need for your murder mystery fund-raising party. Only add the necessary items needed for your fund-raising party. See Sample 2.

Step 5

Make a budget.

Keeping a budget planner is a good idea, especially when you want to put more money toward your charity of choice. See Sample 3.

Step 6

Advertise your murder mystery party.

As soon as you know how many people you can invite, depending on your game or script, let your friends know what you're planning. Let them know that you're raising money for a nonprofit organization.

Step 7

Send the invitations.

When you send out an invitation, the invitation will have an assigned character from your game. It will also include a list of all the guest character parts and will suggest what kind of costume to wear to the party. Be sure to include a response card with the invitation. This way you will know if that person will be participating in your party. This will give you enough time to assign the game's character to someone else if that person is not able to make it. Also, ask your guests to pay for their seat as they respond to your party. See Sample 4.

Step 8

Plan for prizes.

Something else to consider for your fund-raiser is to have prizes for your guests. You can choose any category such as best costume, most valuable player, best role player, and most outrageous accent. Have your guests vote for all of these categories. Make a box into which your guests can drop their votes. The prizes themselves might be a simple certificate, a box of chocolates, or something more suited to the game itself.

Step 9

Send the money!

Send your check or money order. Do not send cash. Also, you can make your contribution at the organization's web site. Do what's best for you.

Step 10

Thank everyone.

Thank your guests by sending them a thank-you note. Express how much fun you had. See Sample 5.

Sample 1—Record Keeping

Charity: Young Audiences—Arts for Learning

Spoke with: Marie Komisar, Director of Development at Young Audiences, Inc.   Date: August 5th

Phone number: 212-831-8110   Contact time: 9:30 a.m.

Web site: www.YoungAudiences.org

E-mail: marie@ya.org

Mailing address: 115 East 92nd St. New York, NY 10128

How will you donate the money? I will make a donation through their web site's online donation section.

Where will you have the party? St. Catherine's School Cafeteria

When will you have the party? Saturday, September 27 from 12p.m.–4p.m.

What game will you play? St. Patty Cakes—Murder Mystery Game

How many people will you invite? 40
On what date will you send the invitations? August 20th
What date will you request all your response cards be sent? September 3rd

Sample 2—Supply List

St. Patty Cakes Murder Mystery Luncheon
Soda pop
Pizza
Chips/dip
Brownies
Ice cream
Bottled water
Napkins
Paper plates
Forks
Paper cups

Sample 3—Budget List

Item	Estimated Cost	Actual Cost
Murder Mystery Game	$24.99	$32.21
Soda pop	$15.00	$16.54
Pizza	$80.00	$88.12
Chips/dip	$20.00	$26.58
Brownies	$10.00	$12.73
Ice cream	$20.00	$19.96
Bottled water	$15.00	$14.32
Napkins	$3.00	$2.26
Paper plates	$3.00	$2.19
Totals	$193.99	$217.37

Sample 4—Invitation/Response Card/Keeping Track

Invitation

St. Patty Cakes' Murder Mystery Game Luncheon
The Headmaster of St. Patty Cakes, Robin Hasher, is pleased to invite you to the school's next Founder's day celebration, commemorating its 150 years of traditions and history.

The celebration will take place on: Saturday, September 27th and start promptly at 12:00 p.m.

The School's address is: 5874 Cardinal Drive,

St. Catherine's School Cafeteria

Please RSVP and return response card to:

Kitty Malone, 490-6492

Your assigned character is:

Brady Yardley, School's Tennis Star.

Costume Recommendation: Tennis Racket, Polo Shirt with Collar Pulled Up.

St. Patty Cakes Who's Who

Most of those are pupils attending St. Patty Cakes. There will also be a handful of staff. Among them will be:

Roger Jenkins—the school's treasurer

Kelly Peking—the school's secretary

Robin Hash—the headmaster

Greg Hash—the headmaster's husband, head of the music department

Henry Burgos—the head boy

Charlotte Ewing—the head girl

Ernie Reynolds—head of science

Delfina Brooks—French teacher

List of Pupils:

Robert Lions—student monitor	Patricia Cates—class snob
Tammy Wallace—most popular girl	Winona Haynes—computer geek
Funny Bill—school clown	Henrietta Janx—best smile
Catherine Bell—nerd	Ida Vines—most likely to succeed
Grant O'Carroll—sneakiest student	Melanie Daniels—most school spirit
Phillip Murdock—most popular boy	Amy Rudolph—school's humanitarian
Teresa Kendrick—most athletic girl	Tracy Rudolph—most talented
Frances Zimmer—class snitch	Barbara Purnell—best dressed
Margot Rydell—friendliest girl	Matthew Andrews—nerd
Peter Finkle—friendliest boy	Brady Yardley—school's tennis star
Leonard Scott—school bully (boy)	Patrick Yardley—computer geek
Penelope O'Hara—most outgoing girl	Phyllis Scott—school bully (girl)
Harry Peters—most athletic boy	Lindsey Rogers—best in band
Ron Gates—most outgoing boy	Mitchell Roberts—most well traveled

Thomas Gates—nerd

Jeffrey Gates—school's soccer star

Ruth Lee—most likely to get into politics

Rebecca Cobb—best dancer

Response Card

You're Invited to a Fund-Raiser Murder Mystery Lunch Party Benefiting Young Audiences—Arts for Learning

www.youngaudiences.org

Please send $20.00 to the address below, along with this card, to reserve your participation before September 3rd. Thank you.

Name:_____

Kitty Malone

4897 Berry Street

Ft. Worth, TX 76101

Keeping Track

Guest	Assigned Character	Will Attend	Amount Paid	Sent Thank you
Terry Powell	Roger Jenkins	Yes	$20.00	❑
Riley Tooley	Kelly Peking	Yes	$20.00	❑
Kari Greer	Robin Hash	Yes	$20.00	❑
Harvey Turkle	Greg Hash	Yes	$20.00	❑
Kurt Wilt	Henry Burgos	Yes	$20.00	❑
Joyce Langley	Charlotte Ewing	Yes	$20.00	❑
Paul Davis	Ernie Reynolds	Yes	$20.00	❑
Lisa Barker	Delfina Brooks	Yes	$20.00	❑
Matt Laolagi	Robert Lions	Yes	$20.00	❑
Kim Garcia	Tammy Wallace	Yes	$20.00	❑
Tim Long	Funny Bill	Yes	$20.00	❑
Katie Vega	Catherine Bell	Yes	$20.00	❑
Eric Keats	Grant OíCarroll	Yes	$20.00	❑
Otis Baird	Phillip Murdock	Yes	$20.00	❑
Heather May	Teresa Kendrick	Yes	$20.00	❑
Tina Waters	Frances Zimmer	Yes	$20.00	❑
Finn Simms	Margot Rydell	Yes	$20.00	❑
Jerome Anthony	Peter Finkle	Yes	$20.00	❑
Doug Baum	Leonard Scott	Yes	$20.00	❑
Janet Kelly	Penelope OíHara	Yes	$20.00	❑

Mark Edlin	Harry Peters	Yes	$20.00	❏
Joe Adler	Ron Gates	Yes	$20.00	❏
Lou Krell	Thomas Gates	Yes	$20.00	❏
Tom Greene	Jeffrey Gates	Yes	$20.00	❏
Tori Frederick	Patricia Cates	Yes	$20.00	❏
Mel Gothia	Winona Haynes	Yes	$20.00	❏
Rachel Cox	Henrietta Janx	Yes	$20.00	❏
Jenny Falling	Ida Vines	Yes	$20.00	❏
Olivia Sweet	Melanie Daniels	Yes	$20.00	❏
Audrey Bibbs	Amy Rudolph	Yes	$20.00	❏
Lauren Connelly	Tracy Rudolph	Yes	$20.00	❏
Kristi McNamara	Barbara Purnell	Yes	$20.00	❏
Chris Montez	Matthew Andrews	Yes	$20.00	❏
Craig Thomas	Brady Yardley	Yes	$20.00	❏
Reece Segal	Patrick Yardley	Yes	$20.00	❏
Eileen Hesler	Phyllis Scott	Yes	$20.00	❏
Sam Greenberg	Lindsey Rogers	Yes	$20.00	❏
Colby Harris	Mitchell Roberts	Yes	$20.00	❏
Suzy Fryman	Ruth Lee	Yes	$20.00	❏
LeAndra Barnes	Rebecca Cobb	Yes	$20.00	❏
Total:			$800.00	

Sample 5—Thank-You Note

Craig,

Thank you for attending my Fund-raising Murder Mystery Party. Everyone had a great time. Your costume was hilariously creative. I guess that's why it was voted best costume by everyone. Thanks again.

Your friend,

Kitty Malone

I am of the opinion that my life belongs to the whole community and as long as I live, it is my privilege to do for it whatever I can. I want to be thoroughly used up when I die, for the harder I work the more I live.—George Bernard Shaw

Activity 9

Sell Plates of Bar-B-Q

Use All Your Proceeds Toward a Charity

This fund-raiser requires a BBQ pit, a hearty appetite, and lots of fun. This fund-raiser can be conducted anytime of year and at any event.

Step 1

How to begin.

Find a local or national charity to donate the funds raised from your Bar-B-Q sales. Get the name of the person you made contact with. Call or e-mail the organization you selected. Tell that person how you plan on earning money for his or her charity. Express how this organization is important to you. Find out what is the best way to transfer the funds: check, money order. Most organizations allow you to make online donations by going to their web site. Always get your parents' permission before making any online donation. You'll need to have a major credit card in order to process your donation. Be sure to get a receipt for your money donation. Refer to www.UltimateVolunteer.com for a listing of nonprofit organizations if you need help deciding which organization you wish to donate to. See Sample 1.

Step 2

Plan a time frame.

What day will you plan on selling your plates of Bar-B-Q? What time of day? Also, plan on selling tickets before the Bar-B-Q. This will help you purchase the Bar-B-Q, potato salad, beans, rolls, pickles, and any other Bar-B-Q menu items you may know. Make sure you stress that they will need their ticket to pick up their plate(s).

Step 3

Map out where you plan on holding your donation drive.

When I was a little girl, volunteers at my church would always sell plates of Bar-B-Q to all of its members to help raise money for new church programs. It was always great timing because I was already hungry after noon mass.

Step 4

How will you package the Bar-B-Q?

You'll definitely need food containers for the Bar-B-Q and utensil packets. You can purchase these types of materials at a wholesale stores such as Sam's Club or Costco.

Step 5

Make a supply list.

Make a list of supplies you'll need for your Bar-B-Q. Only add the necessary items needed for the fund-raiser. See Sample 2.

Step 6

Make a budget.

It's very important to keep a budget planner, mainly because you'll want to put more toward your charity of choice. See Sample 3.

Step 7

Advertise your event.

Tell everyone! Have your aunts and uncles sell tickets to their friends and coworkers. Have your parents sell tickets to their friends and coworkers. Walk door-to-door, sell tickets to people who live in your area. Sell tickets to your teammates and their parents. Sell tickets to members of your church. See Sample 4.

Step 8

Keep track.

Keep track of how many plates you've sold. This is very important because you can't run out of food for this event. When you get a final count, figure out how much meat you'll need for your Bar-B-Q. Ask a local butcher. See Sample 5.

Step 9

Send the money!

Send a check or money order to your nonprofit organization. Never send cash. Most nonprofit organizations have a link to pay online through their web site. Do what's best for you.

Step 10

Thank everyone.

Make a banner that reads "Thank You" to post at your event. As people pick up their plates, they can read the banner that expresses how grateful you are that they purchased a plate of Bar-B-Q.

Sample 1—Record Keeping

Charity: Wheels for Humanity

Spoke with: David Richard Date: April 3rd
Phone number: 818-255-0100   Contact time: 1:30 p.m.
Web site: www.WheelsForHumanity.org
E-mail: Drichard@wheelsforhumanity.org
Mailing address: 12750 Raymer Street, Unit 4, North Hollywood, CA 91605
How will you send the money? I will mail a check to their mailing address.
Why is it important to donate to this organization? I feel that it is important to help those who cannot get around so freely. I can't imagine not being able to walk and not having a wheelchair to help me get around, being independent.
What day will you sell the plates of Bar-B-Q? Saturday, May 6th
Where will you sell the plates of Bar-B-Q? The Glendale's Union
What time will your event take place? 11 a.m.—3 p.m.
How much will you sell each ticket for one plate of Bar-B-Q? $10.00

Sample 2—Supply List

Food container
Plastic fork/knife/napkin/salt & pepper combo
Plastic gloves for food handling
Food handlers permit
Bar-B-Q pit
Potato salad

Beans
Bread
Pickles
Sausage
Chicken
Meat
Bar-B-Q sauce

Sample 3—Budget

Item	Estimated Cost	Actual Cost
Food containers	$25.00	$30.31
Plastic fork/knife/napkin/ salt & pepper combo	$19.99	$25.47
Plastic gloves for food handling	$5.00	$5.86
Food handlers permit	$25.00	$25.00
Potato salad	$50.00	$46.22
Beans	$30.00	$18.19
Bread	$25.00	$17.91
Pickles	$8.00	$10.77
Sausage	$100.00	$110.88
Chicken	$50.00	$47.26
Meat	$100.00	$92.66
Bar-B-Q sauce	$25.00	$32.10
Totals:	$462.99	$462.63

Plates Sold:	$1580.00
Item Total:	($462.63)
Profit:	$1117.37

Sample 4—Ticket Stub

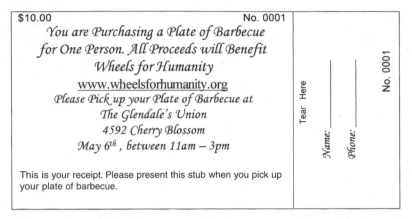

This portion of the ticket stays with the person purchasing the plate of Barbecue.

This portion stays with you for keeping track of those purchasing plates.

Sample 5—Keeping Track

Name	Ticket No.	Arrived?	Amount
Tom K.	0001/0002	Yes	$20
Sue R.	003	Yes	$10
Dan P.	0004/0005	Yes	$20
Jane T.	0006	No	$10
Henry	0007/0008/0009	Yes	$30
Kite E.	0010	Yes	$10
Lisa W.	0011	Yes	$10
Paul C.	0012/0013	Yes	$20
Becky L	0014/0015	Yes	$20
Gary S.	0016/0017	Yes	$20
Ollie V.	0018	Yes	$10
Marc M.	0019/0020	Yes	$20
Inez D.	0021	Yes	$10
Lou B.	0022/0023	Yes	$20
Ken Y.	0024	Yes	$10
Kay G.	0025/0026/0027	Yes	$30
Bo T.	0028	Yes	$10

Jane M.	0029/0030	Yes	$20
Kate H.	0031/0032	Yes	$20
Pete B.	0033/0034	Yes	$20
David R	0035	Yes	$10
Cathy V	0036/0037	Yes	$20
Ida F.	0038/0039	Yes	$20
Hal J.	0040/0041/0042	Yes	$30
Dan T.	0043	Yes	$10
Vicki L.	0044/0045	Yes	$20
Bob R.	0046/0047/0048	Yes	$30
Bill D.	0049	Yes	$10
Lupe L.	0050/0051	Yes	$20
Myra G.	0052	Yes	$10
Tate S.	0053/0054	Yes	$20
Ruth H.	0055/0056	Yes	$20
Eric K.	0057/0058	Yes	$20
Zach P.	0059/0060/0061	Yes	$30
Will Z.	0062/0063	Yes	$20
Fred T.	0064	Yes	$10
Vic R.	0065/0066	Yes	$20
Doug N.	0067/0068	Yes	$20
Greer H	0069	Yes	$10
Mike K.	0070/0071	Yes	$20
Fred C.	0072	No	$10
Linn V.	0073/0074	Yes	$20
Trista T.	0075/0076/0077	Yes	$30

I am only one, but I am one. I cannot do everything, but I can do something.
And I will not let what I cannot do interfere with what I can do.
—*Edward Everett Hale, Author*

Activity 10

Hold a Raffle

Donate the Proceeds Toward a Charity

Everyone loves a raffle. Be sure to be very creative when it comes to the winning prize.

Step 1

How to begin.

Find a local or national charity to donate the funds raised from your raffle sales. Call or e-mail the organization you've selected. Get the name of the person you made contact with. Tell that person about your raffle. Tell him or her why you chose this organization. Find out the best way to transfer the funds: check, money order. Most organizations allow you to make online donations by going to their web site. Always get your parents' permission before making any online donation. You'll need to have a major credit card in order to process your donation.

 Be sure to get a receipt for your money donation. Refer to my Web site at www.UltimateVolunteer.com for a listing of the nonprofit organizations if you need any help deciding which organization you wish to donate to. See Sample 1.

Step 2

Plan a time frame.

When and where do you plan on holding your raffle? How many weeks before will you sell the raffle tickets? I suggest you sell the tickets four weeks before the drawing. That way you have more time to raise money.

Step 3

Map out where you plan on holding your raffle.

Where will you announce the winner(s) of your raffle? Make sure you have a portable microphone to announce the winner. Think of a busy place like a bowling center, a local business, a bingo hall, a mall, or a sporting event. Be sure to get permission from a manager or business owner.

Step 4

Contact businesses.

Start making phone calls to various businesses. Ask them to donate something from their store for your raffle. Give them the name of your contact person of the organization for which you're trying to raise money. Make a list of shops that you think might donate to your cause. See Sample 2.

Step 5

How will you be packaging the item(s)?

Know that whatever you raffle, you'll need to be prepared to have it wrapped with proper packaging. For example, if you're raffling off a stereo, you'll need the box and packaging that comes with it. If the person is not present, be sure to call that person and make arrangements for him or her to pick up the prize.

Step 6

Supply list.

Make a list of items that you'll need for your raffle. See Sample 3.

Step 7

Advertise your raffle.

Sell raffle tickets to everyone! Set up a table at a designated space and display the item or items to show people what they're trying to win. If you have several items, place an empty decorated coffee can in front of each item for people to make their bid. Invite your family and friends to participate. Be sure to announce the drawing date and time to each person purchasing a raffle ticket.

Step 8

Keep track.

Keep track of which business donated what. Also when you display the items, put a courtesy card that reads, "Generously donated by the company." This will also advertise their business. See Sample 4.

Step 9

Send the money!

Send a check or money order. Never send cash. You can also make a contribution through the organization's web site. Every nonprofit organization has a link to donate to their charity.

Step 10

Thank everyone.

Send a big thank-you note to the businesses that donated their merchandise. Without them, your raffle wouldn't have been such a huge success. See Sample 5.

Sample 1—Record Keeping

Charity: Children of Uganda

Spoke with: Robert Alberts, Executive Director   Date: September 25th
Phone number: 214-824-0661 or 800-531-9612   Contact time: 3:30 p.m.
Web site: www.uccf.org
E-mail: rob@childrenofuganda.org
Mailing address: Children of Uganda, P.O. Box 140963, Dallas, TX 75214
How will you donate the money? I will fill out the donation form that Children of Uganda's web site offers and send a check by mail.
Why is it important to you to donate to this organization? There is an orphan crisis in Uganda. Nearly 1 million of children who are under the age of 15 have lost their parents to AIDS. I can't imagine growing up without a mom or dad or both, I want to do everything I can to help.
Where will you have your raffle? At the local bingo hall
Contact Person: Deacon Porter   Phone number: 783-8932
On what dates will you have your raffle? October 10th—October 18th
How much are you selling each raffle ticket? $1.00

Sample 2—List of Businesses

Company: Sears Roebuck and Company
Manager: David Arnold   Phone number: 248-2445
Address: 6022 Crawfordsville Rd.
Will they donate merchandise from their store? Yes

Company: Pier 1 Imports
Manager: Kelsey Kemsley   Phone number: 783-2513
Address: 6810 S Emerson Ave #A
Will they donate merchandise from their store? Yes

Company: Target
Manager: John Murphy   Phone number: 787-9357
Address: 3700 S. East St.
Will they donate merchandise from their store? Yes

Company: Wal-Mart
Manager: Marcus Ortiz   Phone number: 895-6016
Address: 8010 East 38th Street
Will they donate merchandise from their store? Yes

Company: Pottery Barn
Manager: Lacy Barnes   Phone number: 815-3740
Address: 8702 Keystone Xing
Will they donate merchandise from their store? Yes

Company: Bed Bath & Beyond
Manager: Bobbi Travors   Phone number: 843-0746
Address: 8655 River Crossing Blvd.
Will they donate merchandise from their store? Yes

Company: Bath & Body Works
Manager: Holly Crawford   Phone number: 578-3298
Address: 6020 E 82nd St.
Will they donate merchandise from their store? Yes

Company: Best Buy
Manager: Nathan Groves   Phone number: 841-0711
Address: 5820 E 82nd St.
Will they donate merchandise from their store? Yes

Company: Dick's Sporting Goods
Manager: Patrick Wynn   Phone number: 576-0300
Address: 6020 E 82nd St.
Will they donate merchandise from their store? Yes

Sample 3—Supply List

Portable microphone
Portable speaker
Spool of raffle tickets
Empty coffee cans
Construction paper to cover coffee cans

Sample 4—Keeping Track

Company Name	Donation	Thank You	Winner Name	Amount Earned
Sears Roebuck & Co.	Portable Crafts man tool box with starter tools	❑	Raymond Wright: 635-9038	$103.00
Pier 1 Imports	Candle set	❑	Sharon Murphy: 787-7483	$76.00
Target	KitchenAid mixer	❑	Carol Donovan: 635-9273	$241.00
Wal-Mart	Digital camera	❑	Tammy Douglas: 787-4278	$61.00
Pottery Barn	Wood and glass display box	❑	Eddie Garza: 783-8846	$137.00
Bed Bath & Beyond	Egyptian cotton towel set	❑	Darby Frederick: 841-2139	$80.00
Bath & Body Works	Basket with bath soap, lotion, and bath gel with loofah	❑	Jennifer Jamison: 635-0583	$82.00
Best Buy	21î television	❑	Neil Miller: 635-6945	$419.00
Dickís Sporting Goods	Croquet set	❑	Phil Spark: 815-0356	$140.00
Total:				$1,339.00

Sample 5—Thank-You Note

To the management and staff of Pier One Imports,

Thank you very much for donating and preparing a beautiful arrangement of your lovely scented candles. I'm pleased to inform you that your donation gift raised $76.00. All the money raised during the two-week-long raffle will be sent to the Children of Uganda. If you or your staff should ever be interested in this most important foundation, you can too make a donation by going to their web site: www.uccf.org. Again, thank you because without your help my raffle wouldn't have been a true success.

Owen Clooney

SECTION THREE

Humanitarian Awareness

Imagine all the people living life in peace. You may say I'm a dreamer, but I'm not the only one. I hope someday you'll join us, and the world will be as one.—John Lennon

Be the change that you want to see in the world.—Mohandas Gandhi

Activity 1

Make a Collage Representing People, Culture, Language, or Religion of a Foreign Place to Educate

This activity is so much fun if you are creative and keep an open mind!

Step 1

Search for a subject.

There are endless subjects of which you could make a collage! As I read through my *National Geographic* monthly subscriptions, I'm so amazed that there are so many people, cultures, languages, and religions with which we share this earth. I love it! Embrace this experience with your research. See Sample 1.

Step 2

Find a location.

Where will you showcase your collage? Do you have a local art center? A children's museum or local college? Wherever you decide, don't underestimate yourself and put 100% into your work. Be proud of expressing awareness for a subject that you choose.

Step 3

Measure your space.

Make sure you write down the measurements of the space you will be using. You want your collage to be appealing to the eye. It shouldn't be too busy and too much; simply make it special and striking, and you will be sure to spread awareness.

Step 4

Research your subject.

After you choose your subject , learn everything there is to know about it. Become an expert. Learn some of the phrases if the people in this culture speak a different language. Have your mom or dad cook a meal the people in this culture normally eats. Take full advantage of this experience. You'll have so much fun if you're fully involved. See Sample 2.

Step 5

Start cutting and pasting.

Be imaginative! Think of unique ideas that will bring attention to your collage. This is not only a collage, it's a work of art.

Step 6

Put your collage together.

Plan a time to put your collage together. You can even cover it to keep the suspense alive until you unveil it at your Cultural Awareness gathering.

Step 7

Invite your friends and family to view your collage.

Send out invitations and celebrate with punch and cookies. Make a toast in celebration of your subject. See Sample 3.

Step 8

Post activity questions.

You can create an interactive collage. Plan on putting true/false or multiple-choice questions, with the answers, someplace on your collage. This will keep your guests learning! See Sample 4.

Step 9

Lead a discussion.

Verbally express why you chose your subject. Ask your guests how they feel about your collage. Remember to always speak from your heart and others will listen.

Step 10

Ask people to spread the awareness.

Thank your guests for coming to your collage. See Sample 5.

Sample 1—Research

Subject: The Parisian Culture

Where did you find your subject? The *National Geographic* magazine

Where will you showcase your collage? At the admissions center of Arnold Community College

What kind of space are they offering you? A display board.

How big is your space? 6' length x 4' height.

Who gave you permission to show case your collage? The Dean of Admissions, Ken Turner.

How long can you show case your humanitarian awareness project? 1 month

Sample 2—Continuing Research

Where is your subject from? Paris, France

What language does your subject speak? French

What kind of food does your subject eat? Tasty country dishes, cold meats, cheeses, ice cream, Mediterranean specialties.

What religions do they worship? Not sure yet.

Does your subject celebrate any special holiday or celebrations? Christmas, New Year, Festival de Saint-Denis, Théâtre de Verdure Festival at the Jardin Shakespeare, Paris Cinéma, Three Days in America: the American entertainment festival, Festival 100 dessus dessous, Foire Saint-Germain, "Paris breathes," International Cinema, Costume and Fashion Festival, Festival du Film Jules Verne.

Are there special landmarks in Paris? The Fiffel Tower, The Notre Dame Cathedral, The Château de Vaux-le-Vicomte, The Arc de Triomphe

Places to visit in Paris? The Louvre Museum, which houses the *Mona Lisa*, the Seine River, the Moulin Rouge, the Paris zoos, the Versailles Palace just outside of Paris, the catacombs of Paris.

Are there any special events in Paris? The Tour de France always ends its last leg in Paris.

Sample 3—Invitation

You are Invited to my Collage Viewing.

Showcasing The Parisian Culture at The Admissions Center of Arnold Community College on March 18, 2007 at 5:00 p.m.

Invitation List

Guest	Invitation Mailed?	Sent "Thank-You" Note
1. Mom and Dad	❏	❏
2. Cousin Miranda	❏	❏
3. Aunt Lola	❏	❏

4. Uncle Rob	❏	❏
5. Junel	❏	❏
6. Polly	❏	❏
7. Aunt Doris	❏	❏
8. Cousin Tori	❏	❏
9. Miles	❏	❏
10. Kammie	❏	❏
11. Olivia	❏	❏
12. Casey	❏	❏
13. George	❏	❏
14. Kyle	❏	❏
15. Randy	❏	❏
16. Luke	❏	❏
17. Josh	❏	❏
18. Liz	❏	❏
19. Nancy	❏	❏
20. Joyce	❏	❏

Sample 4—True/False Questions

1. The Mona Lisa is at The Louvre museum. T or F
2. The Parisians like outdoor open-air cafés. T or F
3. The Moulin Rouge is only 50 years old. T or F
4. You can take a beautiful boat ride down the Seine River. T or F
5. 3 million people live in Paris, France. T or F
6. The Parisians speak French. T or F
7. You cannot ride a bike in Paris. T or F
8. Paris has 180 museums and monuments for your enjoyment. T or F
9. Paris is known as the "City of Lights." T or F
10. Marie Antoinette was born in Paris, France. T or F

Sample 5—Thank-You Notes

Aunt Lola,

Thank you for attending my Parisian Culture Collage. It turned out to be a hit! I hope you will spread your new found awareness about the Parisians and their culture to others.

Harlow Vaughn

Life's most persistent and urgent question is, "What are you doing for others?"
—Martin Luther King, Jr.

Activity 2

Invite a Police Officer to your School

Ask him or her to discuss the dangers children face today.

This activity is very important. All children need to know the facts they face in today's society. Be the person who could change a person's life with helpful information.

Step 1

Make contact with a police officer.

If you don't know any police officers, head down to your local police station and ask the Chief of Police if he or she has anyone that specializes in teaching children the dangers that they face today.

Step 2

Find a location.

Where will you have your discussion? You can hold your discussion anywhere: your school, the mall, at your home. I bet your classmates would love to meet and listen to a police officer. When I was in fourth grade, our principal had a police officer come to our auditorium to speak to us about safety precautions. It was great. We were able to tour his police car. I still remember his visit, and I'm so happy that he came to our school. See Sample 1.

Step 3

Who will be your audience.

Your audience doesn't have to be only your classmates or your family. You could have your discussion at a local mall, with permission from the mall manager, of course. Advertise your event in advance. Spread the word as much as possible. Each child who listens is a child you can help educate.

Step 4

Research your subject.

What are the dangers children face today? Make a list of possible dangers. I'm sure your mom or dad can help you add to your list. Have questions ready to ask the police officer. Be prepared to cover all possibilities such as length of speech, current issues in the news, etc. See Sample 2.

Step 5

What will you need.

Ask the police officer what he or she will need to have a successful discussion. A microphone will probably be necessary. Don't forget a table for any materials the police officer may offer. See Sample 3.

Step 6

Make a display board.

Find a location for your display board. If your discussion is at school, find a space to post necessary safety material of which children should be aware. If your discussion is elsewhere, you will have to talk to your parents about buying a display board used for science projects. This is perfect to show your efforts of educating children about safety.

Step 7

Create a badge, certificate, or poster.

This is a great way to make everyone feel that they were apart of this learning experience. First, check with the police officer to see if he or she will hand out free stickers or certificates. Some police departments have these on hand. If not, be creative and make them yourself. You could also make a poster and have everyone who attended sign it. See Sample 4.

Step 8

Create an activity.

Create fun games to play during your discussion. You could also make a skit showcasing a lesson children should learn about the dangers they face. Have your mom or dad, brothers, or sisters participate. Kids love visual exercises! You can be sure that your guests will learn a lot. See Sample 5.

Step 9

Opening speech.

Introduce yourself and your guest speaker. Write a speech about why you felt it was necessary to bring everyone together and promote the dangers children face today. See Sample 6.

Step 10

Ask people to spread the awareness.

Come up with a nifty saying or catchphrase. Encourage others about being safe and sound.

Sample 1—Record Keeping

Where will you have the discussion? My guest will hold his discussion in my school's cafeteria.

Who will be speaking to your class? Officer Maxwell from the Police Department.

When will Officer Maxwell speak? October 3rd

What time will your guest arrive and leave? Officer Maxwell will arrive at 9 a.m. and will have an hour to speak.

Who will be your audience? Officer Maxwell will speak to the entire school.

Who gave you permission to have Officer Maxwell speak to the school? Principal Brown

Sample 2—List of Possible Dangers

Speaking to strangers, Internet predators, walking alone to and from school, using the bathroom alone in a public place, accepting anything from a stranger, being outside at night, selling cookies or a product alone, swimming in a pool, lake, stream, or ocean alone, riding in a car without your seatbelt, not wearing your bike helmet or fluorescent belt when riding your bicycle, accepting drugs from anyone, leaving your house doors unlocked, opening the front door without your dad or mom present.

Sample 3—Materials Needed for Guest Speaker

1 heavy duty table
Microphone and speaker

Sample 4—Create a Badge, Certificate, or Poster

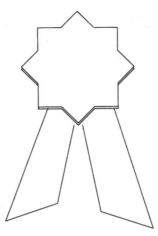

Sample 5—Create an Activity

Skit performed during the discussion.

Two neighborhood friends, Bob and Carmen, are playing outside in their front yard alone. What do they do when a stranger approaches them?

> Bob: What do you want to do next?
> Carmen: I don't know, maybe we can walk to the park.
> Bob: My mom won't let me walk to the park alone.
> Carmen: You won't be alone silly, I'll be with you.
> Bob: I mean with an adult.
> Carmen: Well then what do you want to do next?
> Stranger: Interrupting conversation. . . . *I'll* drop you off at the park.
> Bob: Runs to his house as he screams!
> Carmen: Runs to her house as she screams!

Sample 6—Introduction Speech to Classmates

Hello. My name is Jayne Byrd, and I'm in Mrs. Henry's fifth grade class. This is Officer Maxwell, he or she is a police officer working for the police department. I've asked Officer Maxwell to speak to us about the dangers kids face today because I felt that it's important to know what to do in any dangerous situation or how to prevent a dangerous situation. Thank you.

Wherever a man turns he can find someone who needs him.—Albert Schweitzer

Activity 3

Learn CPR and First Aid

Make others aware of how important it is to know life-saving techniques.

Step 1

Find a guest speaker and trainer.

The best way to learn about first aid is to take a certified first-aid course through your local chapter of the American Red Cross. A basic first-aid training course is offered for kids ages 8 to 12. It teaches all the basic first-aid techniques, including rescue breathing and the Heimlich maneuver, as well as safety on your bike and on the playground. There are other courses for kids over the age of 12, where you can learn advanced life-saving techniques such as CPR (cardiopulmonary resuscitation). Visit the American Red Cross web site at www.redcross.org

Step 2

Find a location.

Where will your training event take place? You'll need to find a spacious area depending on the amount of people who will be attending. The American Red Cross might have a training facility already established. Ask your contact person. See Sample 1.

Step 3

Who will be your audience?

Invite the public and use flyers to promote your upcoming training session. Learning CPR and first aid should be a must for people of all ages. In most states, it's a requirement that kids or teenagers be certified in CPR and first aid to babysit. Make sure to advertise your event. Have people sign up for the course so you and the trainer know how many people will be attending. See Samples 2 & 3.

Step 4

Research your subject.

Learn as much as you can about survival techniques. Take plenty of notes to have all the information you need for your display board.

Step 5

Supply list.

Find out what is needed for your event. Do you need to provide floor mats? Maybe a dry erase board? Ask your mom or dad if they can help you set up a table with refreshments for the event. See Sample 4.

Step 6

Make a display board.

Find a location for your display board. Add important information. Be creative and have fun.

Step 7

Get your card.

Be sure to have the American Red Cross issue certification cards for everyone.

Step 8

Make up scenarios.

Ask the trainer if your group could role-play. Make up cards with real emergencies listed on them. Role-playing may help you prepare for a real emergency. Hopefully no one will have to use his or her CPR or first aid skills; but if you witness a pretend emergency, it will help you prepare for a real one. See Sample 5.

Step 9

Lead a discussion.

Form a circle at the end of the training. Have each person express what he or she liked most about the training. Ask them to spread the awareness of being certified in CPR and first aid.

Step 10

Thank everyone for attending and becoming certified.

Show your appreciation to those who received his or her training. Thank everyone for making a conscientious effort to learn how to use CPR and apply first aid.

Sample 1—Record Keeping

Where will the training event take place? At the Holy Cross church hall
Who will be the trainer for the training course? Alexis Monroe & Julia Parks
When will the training course take place? Saturday, August 11th
How many people can attend the training course? 25
How much does the course cost? $45.00
Are there any discounts for a group? No
Contact person at Holy Cross Church? Olga Cavanaugh
Contact number: 567-8992
Additional information: Church requests that hall be cleaned after use.

Sample 2—Flyer

Learn First Aid and CPR
Certification Course is being offered by The American Red Cross at The Holy Cross Church Hall on Saturday, August 11th
9:00 a.m.—5:00 p.m. Course Fee $45.00
Please contact Joshua Heart at Joshua.Heart@email.com to sign up for the course. Course is limited to 25 persons.

Sample 3—Sign-Up List

1. Blanca Rodriguez
2. Taylor Mathias
3. Frederick Hollars
4. Greg Martin
5. Helen Corns
6. Kim Hughes
7. Margaret Barker
8. Julienne Gonzalez
9. Oliver Fry
10. Piper Marshall
11. Rebecca Lisle
12. Humphrey Brown
13. Carl Small

14. Earl Swartz
15. Quinn Daniels
16. Chris Vickers
17. Tanya Nunn
18. Zena Brush
19. Lyle Jimenez
20. Peter Teeter
21. Ellen McGhee
22. Kindle Thompson

Sample 4—Supply List

1. Table for refreshments
2. Punch
3. Water
4. Animal Crackers
5. Chocolate chip cookies
6. Floor mats
7. 2 tables for the instructors' gear

Sample 5—Emergency Scenarios

Scenarios Typed on Index Cards

A 1 year old baby that you're babysitting for
is choking on a carrot.
What do you do?

Your friend accidentally steps on a rusty nail in her backyard.
Her parents aren't home.
What do you do?

You discover your grandfather passed out on the floor.
What do you do?

You're skate boarding with your friend and he falls, hits his head, and
becomes unconscious.
What do you do?

Kindness is the language which the deaf can hear and the blind can see.
—Mark Twain

Activity 4

Learn about Deaf Culture

Communicating is the spirit of the deaf community. Learning about deaf culture will increase knowledge and awareness.

Step 1

Interview a person who is deaf.

Communicate with a person who is deaf. I took a deaf culture class in college, and the first words that came out of my deaf professor's hands, as she stood next to the chalk board with the sentence already written out, was that, "deaf people do not feel that they are disabled; being deaf was a culture in itself." As the semester went on, I realized that deaf culture was truly a fascinating culture. They are very proud of their language. Take a look at Gallaudet University www.gallaudet.edu. It's a university for people who are deaf. All their courses are taught in sign language. See Sample 1.

Step 2

Visit your local deaf center.

Volunteer at your local deaf and hard-of-hearing center, or take a tour of the facility. You'll be amazed at all the learning opportunities it has to offer.

Step 3

Learn sign language.

Find out if there are any beginning sign language courses you can take. Learn the alphabet. Carry a chart of the alphabet with you for extra help. I learned the alphabet before learning words and phrases. I felt that if I didn't know how to sign a word, at least I could spell out a word. Also, sign language is considered a foreign language. Any sign language learned is only a benefit for you and can open up doors to employment. See Sample 2.

Step 4

Speak to an ear, nose, and throat physician.

Learn as much as you can about the ear parts. Ask the doctor why people are born deaf or how people become deaf. Find out how you can protect your hearing.

Step 5

Experience the culture.

Find out what it would be like to be a part of the deaf culture. Use earplugs or cotton balls to put in your ears to mute sounds. You could possibly ask your family to participate in this project. At home, do not use words to communicate. If you watch television, put the sound on mute. Use sign language or carry some paper around to communicate with others. Write down your experience in your journal.

Step 6

Keep a journal of your culture experience.

Write all your experiences down on paper. Express your feelings about how learning about deaf culture has changed you and how you now view this culture differently.

Step 7

Host a party.

Ask your mom and dad if you could have 6–8 friends over for your party. Don't forget about your new friends from the deaf and hard-of-hearing center. You don't have to make it a big event, just invite 6–8 people.

Step 8

Plan on making a toast using sign language.

Celebrate your new friendships by making a toast using sign language. Your new deaf friends will really appreciate the effort you've made to learn their language. It doesn't matter if it's not perfect; it's the effort you make that counts. See Sample 3.

Step 9

Make a poster board with information about deaf culture.

As you meet people who are deaf or hard-of-hearing, ask them if you could conduct a brief interview. Take pictures of them.

Use pictures of hands forming sign language words to carry out some of your messages. Have fun and be creative!

Step 10

Express your gratitude.

Remember to send a thank-you note to the people that you've interviewed. Promise to remain in contact with your new friends. See Sample 4.

Sample 1—Interview Questions

What is your name?

Where are you from originally?

Were you born deaf?

Are either of your parents deaf?

Are any other family members deaf?

Does your whole family know sign language?

Are you a part of any organizations with other hard-of-hearing or deaf people?

What do you like to do in your spare time?

What school do/did you attend?

Do you know how to read lips?

Sample 2—Minichart of the Sign-Language Alphabet

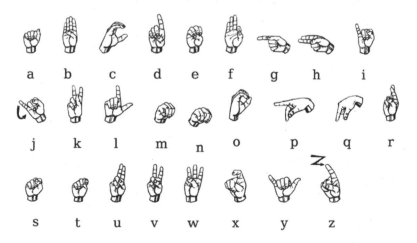

Sample 3—Toast

I would like to take this opportunity to thank my new friend for educating me about deaf culture. This experience has led me to the beginning of learning a new language and becoming aware of new social, cultural, and educational activities.

Sample 4—Thank-You Note

Dear staff and members,

I would like to thank you for teaching me so much about the Deaf and Hard of Hearing Center. I will continue to learn more about deaf culture and become more fluent with sign language.

Sincerely,

Fran Jenkins

Commit to be fit.—Author Unknown

Activity 5

Promote Fitness and Challenge Others

There are lots of ways to be fit. Everyone needs physical fitness to build strength, coordination, and confidence and to lay the foundation for a healthy lifestyle down the road. Exercising promotes stronger bones, a healthier mind, and it keeps your heart in good shape and builds strong muscles and flexibility.

Step 1

What kind of fitness challenge will you have?

Decide on what kind of event you want to have. Will you have a jump rope challenge? A hula hoop challenge? A jumping jacks challenge? Decide on what the challenge will be and make notes. See Sample 1.

Step 2

Where will you hold your event?

Ask your principal or a local fitness club if you could use their facility. Possibly think about using an outdoor basketball court if the weather permits. You'll need lots of space for your fitness challenge.

Step 3

Who will you ask to participate?

Ask your friends and family to come to your challenge and invite the entire student body. Let everyone know how fun and important your event will be. Have people commit themselves to the challenge. Hand out sign-up forms with a detailed explanation of the event. Make sure kids get their parents' permission to participate in the event. See Sample 2.

Step 4

Research important information about your event.

If your event is a jumping jacks challenge, for example, find out how jumping jacks can improve your health. Learn the benefits of exercising and find fun facts about jumping jacks you can share. For example, who holds the record for doing the most jumping jacks? See Sample 3.

Step 5

Supply list.

Make a list of supplies needed for the event. Where will you get your exercise equipment? Can your school supply you with enough jump ropes or hula hoops? If you cannot borrow equipment, choose a challenge that requires only calisthenics, like jumping jacks, sit-ups, lunges, or push-ups. See Sample 4.

Step 6

Make a display board and advertise.

Be creative and make a display board that gets people excited about fitness.

Step 7

Invite a local sports writer or your local news station.

A fantastic way to promote fitness is by promoting it on a wider scale. Nothing could be better than to have the interest of your local news station! Have them broadcast your event, or ask your local sports columnist to write an article in the newspaper. It wouldn't hurt to invite these types of media to your event. The more exposure, the better! See Sample 5.

Step 8

Give a speech at your event.

Let everyone know how much fun you've had and end your speech with an oath to continue to make exercising a part of your life. You want to encourage others! See Sample 6.

Step 9

Hand out awards.

Hand out ribbons or certificates to all participating persons. This is a great way to reward those who worked very hard to challenge themselves. Perhaps include an oath on the certificate and have them sign it to remember each day how important fitness is.

Step 10

Thank everyone for participating.

Thank your mom or dad for helping with your event and thank everyone else for participating. Express your appreciation in your speech.

Sample 1—Record Keeping

What kind of fitness challenge will you have? Hula Hoop challenge
Where will you hold the fitness challenge? At my school's gym
On what day will the fitness challenge be? Saturday, April 15
What time will the event take place? 9:00 a.m.—1:00 p.m.
Who gave you permission for your fitness challenge location?
Principal, Dr. Lisa Goode

Sample 2—Permission Form

I _____ give permission for my son/daughter _____ to participate with the Hula Hoop Challenge. Should an accident or other medical emergency occur during the activity, and neither I nor any other parent or guardian of my son/daughter can be reached for medical authorization, I hereby consent to such hospitalization or treatment, including injections, anesthesia, surgery, and medication, as may be necessary under the circumstances or as may be recommended by medical authorities. I agree to be responsible for all debts that are incurred by my son/daughter during the activity, and for all the expenses not covered by insurance that are incurred as a result of any accident, illness, or medical emergency involving my son/daughter.

Parent/Guardian signature: _____

Date: _____

Printed name: _____

Phone number where you can be reached during the day:

_____

Cell phone number: _____

Health insurance company & policy number:

_____

Doctor's name and phone number:

_____

Medical problems and/or medications your child is currently taking:

Sample 3—Fun Facts

The hula hoop is an ancient invention—no modern company or inventor can claim that he or she invented the first hula hoop. The original hula hoops were made from metal, bamboo, wood, grasses, and vines.

Wham-O is the most successful manufacturer of hula hoops in modern times, and the company that trademarked the name *Hula Hoop* started manufacturing the toy out of the plastic Marlex in 1958.

Twenty million Wham-O hula hoops sold for $1.98 in the first six months.

Sample 4—Supply List

Hula Hoops provided by the school
Tables (for refreshments)
Bottled water
Granola bars
Chairs

Sample 5—Invitation to Local Sports Writer & News Station

Dear _____,

I would like to invite you to a Hula Hoop challenge happening at Wilson Elementary on Saturday, April 15th from 9:00 a.m.—1:00 p.m. This event is to promote health and fitness.

Sincerely,
Edward Valdez

Sample 6—Speech

Hello, everyone. I'd like to thank you for attending the Hula Hoop Fitness Challenge! I'm so glad you're here, to share my enthusiasm for health and fitness.

After we complete today's Hula Hoop Challenge we'll have refreshments in the back of the gym.

Don't think of organ donations as giving up part of yourself to keep a total stranger alive. It's really a total stranger giving up almost all of themselves to keep part of you alive.—Author Unknown

Activity 6

The Living Organ Bank

Start an Awareness Campaign and Promote Organ Donation

Organ and tissue donation is truly a gift of life. Most organs and tissues are donated from individuals at the time of their passing. Organs and tissues that can be transplanted include the kidneys, corneas, heart, lungs, liver, pancreas, heart valves, bone, bone marrow, and skin.

Step 1

Contact the Organ Bank.

Let them know that you want to volunteer. You'll need to fill out a form that you can download from their web site: www.livingbank.org. After they have received your form, they will send you important information concerning organ donation. Your volunteer title for the Organ Bank will be an Organ Bank volunteer. See Sample 1.

Step 2

Get trained.

Once you've received your Organ Bank volunteer training manual, read it and practice how you would relay the information to people. The more information you retain, the easier it will be to answer questions. Be sure to make notes.

Step 3

Speak to your family about the Organ Bank.

Explain the process of organ donation and show them the statistics of people waiting for organ transplants. Ask them if they would like to become an organ donor.

Step 4

Plan a presentation(s) to a club or group.

Set up a time with an organization or members of a club to speak with them about organ donation. Make a contact list of clubs and groups in your area. Call each one. See Sample 2.

Step 5

Setup an exhibit at a health fair or blood drive event.

Be sure to have enough flyers and donor forms on hand.
Also, find out if there are other local Organ Bank volunteers in your area. If so, plan on setting up an exhibit with other volunteers.

Step 6

Contact the local media.

Call your local news station and newspaper to promote organ donation. Show them the statistics and how many people are waiting for organ transplants. Share with them a donor or transplant story.

Step 7

Arrange to place displays in business offices.

Make a list of all the business offices that will allow you to display your awareness of organ donation. Find out what kind of space you will have at each business office. See Sample 3.

Step 8

Work on your displays.

Once you know what kind of space you'll have at each business, you can now make a list of needed supplies. Remember to measure your space and have fun with your displays.

Step 9

Send any new donor forms to the Organ Bank.

As you speak to people, let them know that you will mail their donor form to the Organ Bank.

Step 10

Thank people for their time.

Show your appreciation in person to those who have taken the time to listen to what you've had to say about the Organ Bank. Also, send thank-you notes to the businesses and clubs who have let you speak to their employees or who have let you set up display boards. See Sample 4.

Sample 1—Record Keeping

When did you contact the Organ Bank organization? On June 7th
How did you contact the Organization? By e-mail
When did you receive your local Organ Bank Volunteer training manual? June 24th

Sample 2—Club and Group Organizations

Organization Contacted		Presentation Date	Number Signed Up	Sent Thank-You
Coastal Bend Blood Center	✓	July 12 @ 10AM	2	✓
State School Driscoll Children's Hospital	✓	July 17 @ 2PM	3	✓
Family Outreach	✓	July 24 @ 9AM	2	✓
Health and Human Services Commission	✓	July 25 @ 11AM	1	✓
United Way Youth Odyssey	✓	July 27 @ 3PM	3	✓
Buccaneer Commission	✓	August 1 @ 9AM	1	✓
Bay Area Fellowship Church	✓	August 3 @ 10AM	4	✓
Camp Fire USA Communities in Schools Literacy Council	✓	August 5 @ 1PM	3	✓

Sample 3—Keeping Track—Display Boards

Organization	Type of Display	No. of New Donors
Girl Scouts Council	Portable display board	14

Odyssey Health Care	Portable display board	9
American Red Cross	Portable display board	27
Methodist Health Care Ministries	Portable display board	11
Vista Care Hospice	Portable display board	4
USO	Portable display board	19
Bay Area Hospital— Human Resource Dept.	Portable Display board	32
Athletic Club	Portable display board	44
Valley View Blood Clinic	portable display board	10
Light House—blind or visual impairment	Portable Display board	6

Sample 4—Thank-You Note

Note to the organizations you spoke with in person:

To the Staff of the Buccaneer Commission,

Thank you for allowing me to speak to you about the importance of organ donation. I understand that this is a personal choice, so I hope I gave you enough information to make that decision.

Thank you,

Sylvester Lee

Note to the organizations that let you set up a display board:

To the Staff of Bay Area Hospital,

Thank you for allowing me to place a display board in your human resource department explaining the importance of organ donation. There have been 32 new people from your staff who have signed up to become organ donors. I truly appreciate you letting me spread awareness of this most important subject.

Thank you,

Sylvester Lee

Blood is that fragile scarlet tree we carry within us.—Osbert Sitwell, Writer

Activity 7

Blood Donation

Blood is needed for emergencies and for people who have cancer, blood disorders, sickle cell anemia, and other illnesses. Some people need regular blood transfusions to live. Imagine if everyone donated blood on a regular basis. Can you imagine what kind of difference that would make?

Step 1

Make contact.

Locate your community blood donation centers. Find out if they have a traveling mobile. Be ready to ask questions and answer questions. See Sample 1.

Step 2

Organize a blood drive.

Who will be your target audience? Do you have a local college or university in your area? Clubs? Groups? When I was a college student, the local blood bank would set up their mobile on campus for any students wanting to donate blood. One of my professors decided to give her students 10 extra points in participation grades if they donated blood. Communicate your idea to organize a blood drive with your target audience. See Sample 2.

Step 3

Learn about blood.

Know the facts about blood donation and be sure to learn all there is to know about blood.

Step 4

Know who is qualified.

Know who can and cannot donate blood. Ask your blood donor center to give you that information.

Step 5

Advertise your event.

Use posters or flyers to promote your blood drive. Ask the blood donor center if they have posters you can use. Remember to remove all the posters after your event.

Step 6

Be innovative.

Think of something creative that will benefit the blood donor center. Create an e-mail contact list of new and regular blood donors. This will help the blood donor center with sending out friendly reminders to donate blood. Also, think about giving lollipops attached to hand-written thank-you notes to all those who have donated blood. The better you make the experience, the better they will feel about their blood donation.

Step 7

Schedule appointments.

Once you have established your target audience, make it convenient for them to donate by scheduling appointments. Ask the staff approximately how long it takes to donate blood, so you don't overlap appointments. If you're using a traveling mobile for your blood donation drive, remember there are a limited number of chairs available. Be ready to schedule appointments for people to come back. See Sample 3.

Step 8

Make a display board.

Add some facts and statistics to your display board. Post your display board where others will see it. Also, post the blood supply level for your region on your display board. You can check this by going to www.americasblood.org.

Step 9

Communicate with others.

Spread the importance of blood donation. Urge other voluntary organizations—such as church groups, Boy and Girl Scout organizations, labor unions, and sports teams—to support and participate in the recruitment of voluntary blood donors because it is an ongoing need.

Step 10

Thank the staff.

Thank the staff for their welcoming spirit and for assisting you with your blood drive. See Sample 4.

Sample 1—Record Keeping

Which blood donor center did you contact? Coastal Bend Blood Center
Do they have a traveling mobile? Yes
How many chairs does the blood center have? 15
How many chairs are in the traveling mobile? 4

Sample 2—Organizing a Blood Drive

Where will you organize your blood drive? Bay Area Junior College
Contact person: Gordon Helper, Dean of Students   Phone number: 457-9087
Contact person: Deborah Graves, Biology Professor   Phone number: 457-8236
Has the clinic approved of using the traveling mobile? Yes
Where will they park? Corner of the parking lot located on east campus
How long will the blood drive be? 4 days; Monday, April 9—Thursday, April 12

Sample 3—Scheduled Appointments

Day 1—Monday, April 9

Client	Chair 1	Chair 2	Chair 3	Chair 4
Robert Parks	8:00—9:00			
Kendra Tisdale		8:30—9:30		
Valerie Barker			8:15—9:15	
Jimmy Stewart				8:00—9:00
Joshua Adams	9:00—10:00			
Oscar Banda		10:30—11:30		
Bailey Yarkin			10:15—11:15	
Lila Ramos				10:00—11:00
Romey Pitt	11:00—12:00			
Peter Sandoval		11:30—12:30		
Campbell Jones			12:15—1:15	

Client	Chair 1	Chair 2	Chair 3	Chair 4
Simon Nixon				12:00–1:00
Jonathan Wiley	2:00–3:00			
Thomas O'Neil		2:30–3:30		
Brian Looney			2:00–3:00	

Day 2—Tuesday, April 10

Client	Chair 1	Chair 2	Chair 3	Chair 4
Sarah Kent	8:30–9:30			
Jerome Murray		8:30–9:30		
Brad Hand			9:00–10:00	
Kenny Love				8:45–9:45
Sam Hart	9:45–10:45			
Vicki Horgan		9:30–10:30		
Deena Monroe			10:15–11:15	
Phillip Finney				10:00–11:00
Isla Garza	11:00–12:00			
Melanie Cain		11:00–12:00		
Carter Harold			12:00–1:00	
Georgia Noon				11:15–12:15
J. R. Campa	2:00–3:00			
Undra Simmons		1:00–2:00		
Rick Dunn				12:30–1:30

Day 3—Wednesday, April 11

Client	Chair 1	Chair 2	Chair 3	Chair 4
Kaila Zach	8:00–9:00			
Neil Dillon		8:15–9:15		
Theresa Banda			8:30–9:30	
Luke Jannone				8:00–9:00
LaToya Mavry	9:15–10:15			
Gill Jenkins		9:15–10:15		
Tawny Ervin			9:30–10:30	
Victor Anderson				9:15–10:15
Elliott Patters	10:15–11:15			
Hailey Roberts		10:30–11:30		
Summer Berry			11:00–12:00	
Tionna Plummer				10:30–11:30
Stanley Billups	1:00–2:00			

Frank Hoover   1:00- 2:00
Xavier Cantu   1:30—2:30

Sample 4—Thank-You Note

To the Staff of Coastal Bend Blood Center,

Thank you very much for assisting me with the blood drive at Bay Area Junior College. It was a successful blood drive, and I hope to continue my volunteer work promoting the importance of blood donation.

Thank you,

Stephanie Salazar

Be kind whenever possible. It is always possible.—Dalai Lama

Activity 8

Volunteer at a Senior Citizens Center

Working with the elderly can bring substantial rewards. Our country is nearing a huge increase of senior citizens. By the year 2030, the Baby Boomers will be between the ages of 66 and 84 and make up approximately 20% of the total population in the United States. There will soon be an increase need of volunteers for this population of people.

Step 1

Make contact.

Locate senior citizen centers in your community. Make a list of ten centers near your home. Call each center and inquire about their volunteer program. Ask questions and be prepared to answer questions about why you would like to volunteer at their center. See Sample 1.

Step 2

Commit yourself.

Give yourself a start date and an end date. Decide to volunteer for at least six months, once a week. You will soon realize that your volunteerism with the seniors will have a positive impact on you and on them. See Sample 2.

Step 3

Plan weekly activities.

People love looking forward to events, whether it's as simple as watching a movie or playing bingo. Schedule a monthly calendar of events. See Sample 3.

Step 4

Supply list.

Write down what supplies you'll need for each weekly event planned. Be resourceful think of events that won't require having to spend too much money. See Sample 4.

Step 5

Get requests.

After your first month of planned events, pass comment cards around the senior citizens center for special requests. Receive feedback from the events. See Sample 5.

Step 6

Advertise the events.

Post flyers at the senior citizens center of your scheduled events. Posting the events will give the seniors something to which they can look forward.

Step 7

Display board.

Make a display board and post pictures of your events.

Step 8

Keep a journal.

Share your thoughts and feelings about your volunteerism with the senior citizens center.

Step 9

Spread the word.

Tell your friends about your volunteer work and invite them to help you with your events. Ask them if they would like to become a volunteer.

Step 10

Thank the senior citizens center.

Thank the director and the staff for helping you with your events. You couldn't have done it without them. Also, thank your mom or dad for helping you set up and supporting you with your volunteer work.

Sample 1—Record Keeping

Senior Center	Manager	Do they have a volunteer program?
1. Berry Senior Center	Beverly Leal	Yes
2. Coral Gables Senior Center	Haviland Greer	Yes
3. Crestview Senior Center	Vicki Zamora	No
4. Sunshine Senior Center	Daniel Martinez	Yes
5. Lake Mary Senior Center	Wilma Valdez	Yes
6. Golden Age Senior Center	Tanya Roscoe	Yes
7. Wales Senior Center	John Coates	Yes
8. Meyers Senior Center	Shelly Baines	Yes
9. Palm Towers Senior Center	Lulu Scott	Yes
10. Mulberry Senior Center	Michael Calloway	Yes

Which senior citizens center did you decide to volunteer with? Sunshine Senior Center

Do they have a volunteer orientation course? Yes

How many senior citizens live at the senior citizens center? 62

Do they have an activity center? Yes

How many people work at the senior citizens center? 16

How many volunteers do they have volunteering at the senior citizens center? 2

Do they currently have activity programs at the senior citizens center? No

Sample 2—Volunteer Schedule

February

Sun	Mon	Tues	Wed	Thurs	Fri	Sat
1	2	3	4	5	6	7
					6—9	10—2
8	9	10	11	12	13	14
6—9					10—2	1—4
15	16	17	18	19	20	21
					6—9	10—2
22	23	24	25	26	27	28
1—4					6—9	10—2

Sample 3—Calendar of Weekly Activities

February

Sun	Mon	Tues	Wed	Thurs	Fri	Sat
1	2	3	4	5	6 Movie Night 1	7 Monthly Birthday
8 Book Reading	9	10	11	12	13 Movie Night 2	14 Valentine's Day
15	16	17	18	19	20 Movie Night 3	21 Game: Bingo
22 Outside Activity: Gardening	23	24	25	26	27 Sock Hop	28 Game: Bridge

Sample 4—Supply List

Movie Nights

1 *Casablanca* DVD	punch	cookies
2 *Gone with the Wind* DVD	peanuts	plastic cups
3 *The African Queen* DVD	popcorn	napkins

Monthly Birthday

Celebration cake	forks	birthday banner
Punch	napkins	
Plates	plastic cups	

Book Reading

The Notebook by Nicholas Sparks
Portable microphone

Valentine Card Making

construction paper	markers
Glue	crayons
Scissors	doilies

Games

Bingo	Bingo cards	Microphone
Bridge	Decks of cards	

Gardening Day

Soil
Flowers
Planters

Sock Hop

Fifties music	Cake	forks
Stereo	Punch	napkins
Plates		

Sample 5—Comment Cards

Which of the following activities did you participate?

❑ Movie Night
❑ Monthly Birthday Celebration
❑ Book Reading
❑ Valentine Card Making
❑ Bingo
❑ Bridge
❑ Gardening Day
❑ Sock Hop

How would you rate this month's social activities?

❑ Very Satisfied
❑ Satisfied
❑ Not At All Satisfied

Which of the following activities would you like to participate with in the upcoming months?

❑ Arts and Crafts
❑ Musical Events
❑ Beauty Days
❑ Exercise Fun
❑ Religious Services
❑ High Tea

Please recommend any other activity that is not listed above:

_____

_____

_____

Friendships born on the field of athletic strife are the real gold of competition.
—Jesse Owens

Activity 9

Volunteer with the Special Olympics

Volunteering with Special Olympics can be a life-changing experience. There are year-round sports training facilities located around the United States.

Step 1

Make contact.

Contact your local Special Olympics program. You can locate a program near you by going to www.specialolympics.org. Use the web sites program finder. See Sample 1.

Step 2

Educate yourself.

Learn about the Special Olympics. Read the *General Orientation Handbook*. The orientation handbook informs you about the Special Olympics' movement, its mission, its history, and, above all else, it's athletes.

Step 3

Eligibility and qualifications.

Whatever your interests, talents, background, and availability, there are volunteer opportunities for you with the Special Olympics. There is event-specific volunteering or year-round volunteering positions available. Speak to your parents about what would be best for you. Take notes. See Sample 2.

Step 4

Try an event.

Take a look at the various sports the athletes perform at the Special Olympics. With help from your parents, try a few of the events yourself.

Can you do them? Are they difficult? Make a list of the ones you're good at. See Sample 3.

Step 5

Big day.

Be committed to your volunteer work and give it your all. If you're unsure about something ask a staff member for help and have fun.

Step 6

Interview the athletes.

Volunteering for the Special Olympics is an honor. It provides you the opportunity to work with some of the most gifted athletes. You will meet athletes that come from different countries and speak different languages. Don't be hesitant to introduce yourself and ask them lots of questions. Make a list of questions before your interviews. See Sample 4.

Step 7

Keep a journal.

What's it like to volunteer with the Special Olympics? Write down all your thoughts and experiences.

Step 8

Make a poster board.

Post pictures of your volunteer work with the Special Olympics and share it with your classmates.

Step 9

Promote the Special Olympics.

Tell your friends and family about your experience with the Special Olympics. If there is not a local program in your area, let the state/provincial or national Special Olympic offices know that you want to contribute to the growth of the movement by starting a local program. Special Olympics has also put together the *Ready, Set, Go! Special Olympics Local Program Development Kit and Guide* to help you and potential Special Olympics athletes become fully involved in the movement. You can download the program by going to their web site.

Step 10

Thank others.

Thank the Special Olympics. Share with them the benefits of volunteering with the Special Olympics. Thank your parents for being supportive throughout your volunteerism. See Sample 5.

Sample 1—Record Keeping

Organization: Special Olympics
Contact person: Lois Arnold
Title: Executive Director   Telephone: (989) 774-3911
Web site: www.somi.org
Location: E. Campus Drive, Central Michigan
                University, Mt. Pleasant, MI 48859

Do you have a program in your city? No, but it's only 21 miles away.

Sample 2—List of Interested Volunteer Positions

Ball shagger
Escort
Set-up/clean-up crew
Food server

Sample 3—List of Special Olympic Sports

I'm Good At:
Aquatics
Basketball
Bowling
Cycling
Football (Soccer)
Golf
Roller skating
Poly hockey
Snow shoeing
Softball
Volleyball

Sample 4—Interview Questions

How long have you been participating in the Special Olympics?
What event(s) do you compete in?
What are your favorite sports?
Who's your favorite professional athlete? Why?
Have you ever placed in an event?
Where are you from?
Did any of your relatives travel here to watch you? Who?

Sample 5—Thank-You Note

To the Office Staff, Volunteers, and Athletes,

I would like to express my sincere appreciation to all those that made my volunteer experience more meaningful. The event wouldn't have been a success if it weren't for everyone involved. I will treasure all the memories.

Thank you,

Justin Rutkowski

Those who can, do. Those who can do more, volunteer.—Author Unknown

Activity 10

Volunteer at a Children's Hospital

The personal satisfaction that comes from making a child's hospital stay a little easier is one of the greatest feelings you'll ever feel. All it takes is your time and lots of compassion.

Step 1

Make contact.

Contact the children's hospital(s) in your area. Find out what kind of volunteer program they offer. See Sample 1.

Step 2

What do you have to offer?

Do you like reading? Do you like painting? Let the children's hospital know what your talents are and what you can do for the kids who are in the hospital.

Step 3

Commit yourself.

Give yourself a start date and an end date. Decide to volunteer for a significant period, for at least six months to a year, once a week. Your commitment will be a valuable asset to yourself and to others.

Step 4

Plan an event.

First, find a location at the hospital for your event and get other volunteers involved with the event. Think of something everyone will enjoy and propose your event to the hospital's director for approval. See Sample 2.

Step 5

Supply list.

What will you need for your event? What can other volunteers do for your event? Ask the hospital to provide refreshments for your event. See Sample 3.

Step 6

Advertise your event.

Post flyers at various hospital wings. Get approval from management to post these flyers. See Sample 4.

Step 7

Get feedback.

After your event, pass out feedback cards to all the children and parents.

Step 8

Keep a journal.

What have you learned as you've volunteered with the children's hospital? Write down all your thoughts and feelings.

Step 9

Spread the word.

Tell your friends and family about your experience with volunteering for the children's hospital. Ask them if they would like to volunteer as well.

Step 10

Be proud of yourself.

Your commitment to children suffering from a temporary or terminal illness is something of which to be proud. You have shown yourself to have the capacity to care and treat others with dignity.

Sample 1—Record Keeping

Hospital Name: Children's Hospital South
Spoke with: Bonnie Sutton, Volunteer Coordinator: August 23rd
Phone number: 222-7530 Contact time: 11:15 a.m.
Do they have a volunteer program? Yes
Do you have to attend a volunteer orientation? Yes
Orientation date? September 9th at 10 a.m.

Sample 2—Event Planner

Who gave you permission for the event? Bonnie Sutton
What type of event? A Puppet Show
Location of event? Waiting Room on Floor 12
Date of event? October 18th
Time of event? There will be two puppet shows. 1st puppet show 10 a.m.
2nd puppet show 2 p.m.

Sample 3—Supply List

Puppet script
Puppets
Other volunteers to manage other puppets
Puppet theater
Cookies
Punch
Plastic cups
Napkins

Sample 4—Flyer

You're Invited to a
Puppet Show
on Saturday, October 18th
First Show 10 a.m.
Second Show 2 p.m.
For More Information Please Contact
Bonnie Sutton, Volunteer Coordinator

SECTION FOUR

Ecological Awareness

Only when the last tree has died and the last river been poisoned and the last fish been caught will we realize we cannot eat money.—Cree Indian Proverb

There is hope if people will begin to awaken that spiritual part of themselves,
that heartfelt knowledge that we are caretakers of this planet.
—Brooke Medicine Eagle, Author and Ecologist

Activity 1

Pick up Litter around your Neighborhood

Plan a Litter Project with your Neighbors

It is very important to preserve the surrounding area you live in by keeping it clean and litter free. It should be everyone's responsibility to pick up
trash and litter anytime and anywhere.

Step 1

Set a time.

Decide on a day and time that works best for you and your family. Make
the time, place, and duration explicitly clear to everyone you tell. See
Sample 1.

Step 2

Contact your neighbors.

Let your neighbors know what you're planning on doing in advance. Leave
a note in their mailboxes. See Sample 2.

Step 2

Invite people.

Organize a neighborhood litter project. As you contact your neighbors
about your litter project, invite them to participate. Ask them to contact
you in advance if they plan on joining your litter project.

Step 4

Keep it simple.

All you need are trash bags, gloves, an outdoor broom, a shovel, and a rake.

Step 5

Keeping track.

Keep track of the type of litter you're picking up. Is your area a dumping ground for a specific waste? See Sample 3.

Step 6

Tell the Press.

Simply call your local newspaper or radio station and tell them the specifics of what you're doing. Even if you are working alone, you will still peak interest, and people may want to join you next time.

Step 7

Keep a journal.

Write down all your experiences with your project. What did you enjoy about your litter project? Would you do anything different?

Step 8

Make a poster board.

Take pictures of your event. Post the pictures to your poster board and show it to your friends at school or post it in your room. You should be very proud of yourself for making a difference in your community.

Step 9

Spread awareness.

Tell others about your litter project. Give them specifics about your event. Express how much fun you had as you made a difference to your community.

Step 10

Thank you.

Send thank-you notes to those who participated with the litter project. Also, thank your parents for their support and help. See Sample 4.

Sample 1—Record Keeping

What day is your litter project with your neighbors? Saturday, May 28th
What time is your litter project? 9:00 a.m.—2:00 p.m.
Where will your litter project take place? Just one block, on Gilligan Street.

Sample 2—Note to Neighbors

Dear Neighbor,

I'm organizing a neighborhood litter project on Saturday, May 28th beginning at 9:00 a.m. I'm hoping that the whole neighborhood will get involved with cleaning our street. Hope to see you then!

Your Neighbor,

Trey Kimmel

Sample 3—Keeping Track

Plastic	Paper	Glass	Regular Trash	Biode-gradable
plastic grocery bag	French fry container	beer bottles	diapers	banana peel
plastic straw and lid	bubble gum wrapper	broken glass		pile of leaves
ketchup packets	fast food paper bag			broken egg shells
	milk carton			
	soda pop box			

Sample 4—Thank-You Note

Dear Neighbor,

Our neighborhood litter project was such a success! Thank you for your participation and effort. Remember picking up one piece of trash everyday will help keep our street looking beautiful!

Your neighbor,

Trey Kimmel

Vegetables are a must on a diet. I suggest carrot cake,
zucchini bread, and pumpkin pie.—Jim Davis, Writer

Activity 2

Learn How to Grow an Organic Vegetable Garden

Growing organically is really good old-fashioned gardening.

Step 1

Learn the importance of organic growing.

Take an organic gardening course to help you get started. If you can't find any courses in your area, contact a local organic garden shop or do your own research by visiting your library or a book store. See Sample 1.

Step 2

Plan your garden.

Decide on what kind of vegetables you plan to grow. Consider your family and make a list of vegetables you like and what your family likes. Grow vegetables that your entire family will enjoy. See Sample 2.

Step 3

Measure your space.

With permission from your parents, take a look at the space you'll be using for your organic vegetable garden. Draw an outline of your garden. See Sample 3.

Step 4

Order your organic products.

Find a garden store that sells organic products or order your products through an online organic garden store. Make a shopping list of desired products. See Sample 4.

Step 5

Supplies.

As you plan your organic garden, plan on making a list of garden tools you'll need for your project. Have your parents help you identify the tools. See Sample 5.

Step 6

Get to work.

Plan the day with your parents to start your organic vegetable garden. Use markers to label your vegetables. Remember to keep the required space between each seed. Refer to your research facts!

Step 7

Keep a journal.

Write all your experiences down on paper. Keep track of how your organic vegetable garden is growing.

Step 8

Enjoy your product.

Enjoy eating the vegetables you've grown! You should be very proud of yourself for growing healthy food. Share them with your family, friends, and neighbors.

Step 9

Make others aware.

Show your garden to your friends, neighbors, and extended family members. Explain the process of your garden and what *organic* means. Ask them to grow an organic vegetable garden.

Step 10

Thank your parents.

Write a thank-you note to your parents for helping you with your vegetable garden. See Sample 6.

Sample 1—Record Keeping

Gardening Course Location: Turner's Gardenland
Course: Organic Gardening Basics Course Fee: Free
Spoke with: Garry Strickland   Date: March 2nd
Phone number: 831-9064 Contact time: 12:45 p.m.
Location: 645 Webber Road, Santa Fe, New Mexico, 87501

Sample 2—List of Vegetables My Family Likes to Eat

Beans
Beet
Broccoli
Cabbage
Carrot
Cauliflower
Celery
Cucumber
Eggplant
Green onion
Lettuce
Potato
Pumpkin
Radish
Spinach
Squish
Tomatoes
Turnips
Watermelon

Sample 3—Outline of the Garden

Sample 4—Order List of Organic Seeds

Carrots
100 seeds, Sows—3' $2.40
Cucumbers
1/16 ounce,—64 seeds, Sows—30' $2.40
Tomatoes
1/10 gram,—30 seeds $2.40

Sample 5—Supply List

Organic soil:
A healthy soil, rich in nutrients and life, is the essential building block of any garden.
Garden gloves:
Use to help from calluses and hand fatigue when using gardening tools.
Spade or spading fork:
Use to turn the ground, to turn under organic matter, and to break up large clumps of soil.
Rake:
Use to smooth out the soil after spading and after preparing the seedbed. You can also use it for clearing up debris and removing small weeds.
Hoe:
Use to remove tough weeds and to cover seeds after planting. When turned sideways, you can also use a hoe to dig a V-shaped row for planting.
Yardstick, twine, and stakes:
Use to get rows evenly spaced and laid out in straight lines.
Putty knife or spatula:
Either one of these items is handy for digging up a growing plant from one location to plant it in another location or is great for cleaning other tools.
Trowel: One of the handiest garden gadgets. It is useful for transplanting and for loosening soil around plants.
Dibble:
Short, round, pointed stick is used to make holes for transplanting seedlings and to firm the soil around the plant roots.
Wheel hoe and attachments:
Use for controlling weeds and for making furrows for deep-seeded crops.

Sample 6—Thank-You Note

Dear Mom and Dad,

I had so much fun planning an organic garden with you! I can't wait to see the seedlings begin to sprout. With lots of love and care, we'll be able to eat the vegetables by this summer.

I love you,

Jennifer Tooley

We do not inherit the earth from our ancestors, we borrow it from our children.
—American Indian Proverb

Activity 3

Learn to Recycle

Encourage Others to Recycle

Recycling makes the world cleaner, and it makes the grass and trees greener, you can recycle glass and cans, clothes and shoes, paper and plastic.

Step 1

Locate your local recycling facility.

If your city doesn't pick up recycling from your driveway, find your local recycling facility. Find out what the drop-off requirements are. See Sample 1.

Step 2

Educate yourself.

Find out what you can recycle. Learn what makes up your household materials. Make a list of items that are paper, plastic, and biodegradable. See Sample 2.

Step 3

Change your life for our earth.

Start now by doing the following: Discontinue using cling film and foil wrap. Use reusable containers instead of plastic baggies. Donate unwanted clothes and household items to charity. Buy milk in returnable glass bottles, instead of plastic containers. Invest in rechargeable batteries.

Step 4

Learn to separate paper, plastics, and compost materials.

Invest in two trash cans: one for paper, and one for plastics. Label your receptacles to make it easy for everyone. Build a compost holding unit for your biodegradable trash.

Step 5

Recycle your textiles also.

Remember you can recycle your clothes, linens, shoes, and handbags. Recycle your textiles by donating them.

Step 6

Become resourceful.

Reuse magazines and newspapers. I remember when I was a little girl it was common to receive a gift wrapped in the comics section of a newspaper. You can also use a regular newspaper and find words to highlight that may describe the person to which you're giving a gift.

Step 7

Make a display board.

Express your knowledge about recycling through your artistic talents. Divide your display board into three sections: Plastic, Paper, and Biodegradable. Post pictures of items that fall under each category. This will help others learn how to separate their recyclables.

Step 8

Conduct a classroom project.

Ask your teacher if you can have a paper recycle can for your classroom. Schools have so much paper thrown away each school year. Speak to your principal about a school-wide paper recycle project.

Step 9

Keep a journal.

How has your experience been with recycling? Do you feel like you're making a difference? How fast does your paper and plastic recycling bin fill up?

Step 10

Tell everyone.

Encourage others to recycle! Explain how easy it is once you start doing it.

Sample 1—Record Keeping

Name of Recycling Center: Mulberry City Recycling Center
Spoke with: Mallory Bradshaw, Client Service Care Specialist   Date: July 15th
Phone number: 753-0142 Contact time: 2:50 p.m.
Mailing address: 6733 Crosswinds, Warrensburg, Missouri 64093
Do they have a pick-up service? No
Can you drop recyclable items? Yes
Hours of Operation: 8 a.m.–5 p.m. M-F: 8 a.m.–12 p.m. Sat
Drop-off Instructions: Plastic and Paper must be separated!

Sample 2—List of Household Recyclable Items

Paper	Plastic, Glass, and Aluminum
milk carton	pickle jar
brown paper bags	soda pop 2 liter bottle
egg cartons	plastic laundry detergent bottle
greeting cards	plastic cleaning bottles (rinsed)
pizza boxes	plastic baggies
wrapping paper	shampoo plastic bottle
newspaper	toothpaste tube
cereal boxes	mayonnaise jar
phone books	mustard plastic container
newspaper	ketchup plastic container
magazines	beer bottles
soda boxes	baby jar container
computer paper	grocery store plastic bags
tissue boxes	plastic hangers
soap boxes	orange juice container
craft paper	potato chip bag
envelopes	plastic wrap around bought food
junk mail	aluminum cans
catalogs	water bottle
file folders	peanut butter jar
gift boxes	aluminum foil
shirt boxes	butter tub plastic container
cracker boxes	yogurt container
toilet paper roll	plastic plant pots
toothpaste box	laundry detergent box

We never know the worth of water till the well is dry.
—Thomas Fuller, Gnomologia, 1732

Activity 4

Clean up Nearby Lake, Stream, Pond, or Ocean Shores

Everyone needs to do their part to keep our shorelines clean each and every day. It very important to save the preservation of our waterfronts for future generations to come.

Step 1

Find a location.

Depending on where your cleanup takes place, it can either be a small, medium, or big undertaking. Choosing your site is really important, so you have to ask yourself how much work to which you're willing to commit. Be sure you choose a cleanup site that is not too big or too challenging for your group. Cleanups are meant to be fun and rewarding, so try and find a clean up site that best suits your group's size and level of commitment. See Sample 1.

Step 2

Learn more about shoreline litter.

Shoreline litter comes in many forms and sizes. It can be wood, plastic, metal, glass, cloth, or paper and can be as small as a plastic resin pellet or as large as a couch. It can cause serious problems for wildlife, ecosystems, and us! Learn as much as you can so that you know how to communicate to others just how important it is to keep our shorelines litter free.

Step 3

Organize a cleanup team.

Your cleanup could include a small number of friends/family/colleagues or the whole community—it's up to you! Set a cleanup date and time and make a list of cleanup activities. See Sample 2.

Step 4

Be committed to your project.

Give it your all. Put 100% effort into your event! Don't stop until your area is cleaned.

Step 5

Be sensitive to your location.

Shorelines are a diverse and important habitat for many plants and animals. However, sometime shoreline litter can become a part of that habitat. If you find a piece of litter that an animal or plant has used as its home, leave it there! Once that bottle, tin can, or car tire has become a home, it is part of the shoreline habitat. In many cases, removing it would do more harm then good.

Step 6

Safety and supplies.

Safety should be every cleanup person's #1 concern. Whether it's an ocean, lake, or river, you are still cleaning up near water, so take the proper precautions. Be especially sure that small children are kept away from the water if unsupervised, and bring a first aid kit just in case. Remind your volunteers to wear gloves, the proper footwear, and to dress for the weather. Make a list of supplies you'll need for your cleanup project. See Sample 3.

Step 7

Have fun!

Come up with prizes, challenges, and time trials for your group. Wear costumes, or even make the cleanup part of a whole series of different activities through the day. The most important part is to enjoy your time cleaning up the shoreline. Having fun is a sure way to get people to join you year after year, and even more, the shoreline will be cleaned! See Sample 4.

Step 8

Contact the media.

The media is always the best way to promote your awareness. Contact your local newspaper or local television station two weeks before your event.

Step 9

Make a poster board.

Take before and after photographs for your poster board. Don't forget to take pictures of your cleanup team. Share it with your family or your classmates.

Step 10

Thank everyone.

Send thank-you notes to your friends and family who participated with the cleanup. Give yourself a pat on the back. You completed a very good project. See Sample 5.

Sample 1—Record Keeping

Clean-Up Site: Mono Lake
Location: Lee Vining, California
Spoke with: Geoff McQuilkin, Director, Mono Lake Committee
    Date: March 8th
Phone number: 760-647-6595   Contact time: 10:30 a.m.
Mailing address: Corner of Hwy. 395 & 3rd Street, P.O. Box 29, Lee Vining, CA 93541
What type of shore? Lake
How big is the shoreline? 57.4 sq. mi

Sample 2—Cleanup Teams

Team 1—Joanna Clarke, 234 Rosebud, Lee Vining, CA 93541, 000-269-1845
    Thomas Clarke, 721 Ruby, Lee Vining, CA 93541, 000-589-6487
    Kevin Hunker, 8934 Tipper, Lee Vining, CA 93541, 000-956-5862
    Mimi Casaras, 8935 Horne, Lee Vining, CA 93541, 000-936-7834
Team 2—Homer Gonzalo, 783 Cotton, Lee Vining, CA 93541, 000-594-8264
    Leslie Parnell, 4354 Baker, Lee Vining, CA 93541, 000-784-7823
    Janet Rothchild, 436 Raven, Lee Vining, CA 93541, 000-856-5647
    Eduardo Rothchild, 436 Raven, Lee Vining, CA 93541, 000-856-5647
Team 3—Warren Kist, 8956 Waverly, Lee Vining, CA 93541, 000-568-5691
    Patsy Bassell, 811 Kay, Lee Vining, CA 93541, 000-569-8216
    Kirsten Hall, 2137 Halliwell, Lee Vining, CA 93541, 000-594-2659
    Michele Best, 8963 Ketchum, Lee Vining, CA 93541, 000-673-3856
Team 4—Olive Rose, 836 Handley, Lee Vining, CA 93541, 000-895-6317
    Lionel Benavides, 782 Trinidad, Lee Vining, CA 93541, 000-893-3723
    Luke Kennedy, 7845 Clarkson, Lee Vining, CA 93541, 000-895-6152

Steve Joiner, 2145 Halliwell, Lee Vining, CA 93541, 000-594-6745
Team 5—My Family
Carl Jung
Barbara Jung
Chastity Jung
Doug Jung

Sample 3—Supply List

(5) First aid kits
Ice chest
Ice
Cups
Napkins
Water
Sandwiches
Chips
Sturdy plastic outdoor trash bags
Colored bandanas for each team:
Team 1—Yellow bandana
Team 2—Red bandana
Team 3—Blue bandana
Team 4—Green bandana
Team 5—White bandana
Prize for reward challenges
Team prize—book about Lake Mono for each member
Ask everyone to wear and bring these items:
Gloves
Protective footwear
Right clothes for the Weather
Sun block
Hat
Sunglasses
One cell phone per team

Sample 4—Cleanup Schedule/Activities

8:00–8:30   Teams will meet at the east shoreline of Lake Mono. Each team will receive a cleanup kit that includes one first aid kit, trash bags, bottled water, and team colored bandanas. Exchange team cell phone numbers.

8:30—8:45   Instructional Overview

8:45—11:45   Shoreline Cleanup with teams

11:45—12:00   Teams will report back to meeting point. Reward challenge prize given to team member who has the most garbage.   .

12:00—1:00   Lunch

1:00—3:30   Shoreline Cleanup with teams

3:30—4:00   Teams report back to meeting point. Teams will be given a True/False questionnaire about Lake Mono, the team with the most correct answers win!

Sample 5—Thank-You Note

Given to each team member and to the Committee of Lake Mono.

To Team member:

Janet,

I would like to thank you for volunteering your time to help cleanup the shoreline of Lake Mono. The day turned out to be a success! Your effort will help preserve Lake Mono for years to come.

Thank you,

Carl Jung

To Committee of Lake Mono:

To the Committee of Lake Mono,

I would like to take this opportunity to thank you for your guidance and assistance to help cleanup Lake Mono. The volunteers had a great time helping to maintain Lake Mono's beautiful landscape. I appreciate your time and hope to work with you on future volunteer work.

Thank you,

Carl Jung

He who plants a tree, Plants a hope.—Lucy Larcom, Writer and Poet

Activity 5

Plant a Tree: Organize a Tree-Planting Project

Trees are very important to our environment. Trees provide essential benefits to our earth. They also bring joy to everyone; you can hang a swing from a tree, you can climb a tree, you can build a clubhouse in a tree, and you can hang a hammock from a tree and enjoy a good book.

Step 1

What are the benefits of trees?

The trees you plant remove carbon dioxide from the air and help fight global warming. They produce oxygen and give songbirds a home. Also, trees that are properly placed around buildings and homes can reduce air conditioning costs and break the cold winds to save energy used for heating. Find out what trees will grow best where you live.

Step 2

Tree placing.

Before you decide to plant your tree, sit down with your parents to discuss where your tree will be planted. It's important to know the types of trees that grow best in your area. Consider utility lines, sun/shade requirements, the width and height the tree will achieve when it reaches maturity, and the type of soil that's best suited for the tree. See Sample 1.

Step 3

Visit your local tree store.

Make a list of all the necessary supplies you will need to plant your tree. Also, keep in mind the time of year you're planting your tree because climate will play an important role in how well your tree grows.

In addition to the weather, digging a proper hole for your tree also plays an important role. Most people make the mistake of digging holes that are too deep and too narrow; this is not how you want to dig your hole. A proper tree hole should be no deeper than the container in which it arrived from the tree store. You should also dig the hole at least three times wider than the container. This will give your tree plenty of oxygen for its roots and will also allow it to establish itself in the ground. See Sample 2.

Step 4

Campaign for a tree planting project.

Now that you have experienced planting your tree, you can start a tree-planting project for your neighborhood, school, or local park. Find an area that is in desperate need of trees and *ask others to donate a tree.* Form a committee for your project. Ask your local tree store if they could give you a better cost, per tree, if you purchase a certain amount of trees. Or better yet, maybe they'll be willing to donate some trees for your project. Don't forget to make a list of those who have committed to donating a tree, they'll be known as your tree donors. See Sample 3.

Step 5

Keeping track.

Keep track of tree donors and tree planters. Plan a day and time for your project. Have your mom or dad help you plan for a table of refreshments. See Sample 4.

Step 6

Plant a tree to honor someone.

To dedicate a tree to someone is probably one of the most ecological friendly and unique presents you can buy. It's a gift that's suitable for all occasions whether it's to celebrate someone's birth, a wedding gift, and or a graduation gift.

Step 7

Keep a journal.

As you take care of your tree and watch it grow, write down how you enjoy having picnics under your tree or how strong your tree is as you climb it. Also, take measurements of your tree's trunk as it grows.

Step 8

Make a display board.

Post your display board at school, at a local club, or maybe your local tree store. Show pictures of different kinds of trees. Explain the anatomy of a tree, which includes the outer bark, the inner bark, the cambium cell layer, sap wood, and the heartwood. Have fun with your display board as you express the importance of trees.

Step 9

Spread awareness.

Share your knowledge of trees to everyone you meet. Make sure you express the importance of every tree that is planted.

Step 10

Thank everyone.

Send thank-you notes to all those that donated trees to your tree-planting project and those that helped plant the trees. Also, thank your parents for helping you with your project. See Sample 5.

Sample 1—Tree Placing Notes

What types of tree grows best in your area? Korean Boxwood (*Buxus microphylla koreana*), Bar Harbor Juniper horizontalis "Bar Harbor", Juniper, Hybrid Poplar (*Populus deltoides x Populus nigra*), Red Maple (*Acer rubrum*), Eastern Rosebud (*Cercis canadensis*), American Holly (*Ilex opaca*), Yellow Poplar Tuliptree (*Populus deltoides x Populus nigra*), Camellia (*Camellia sasanqua*), Leyland Cypress (*X Cupressocyparis leylandii*), Saucer Magnolia (*Magnolia x soulangiana*)
Are there any utility lines around your house? No
Are there trees already planted around your house? No
What types of trees will you and your family plant? Yellow Poplar Tuliptree (*Populus deltoides x Populus nigra*), Hybrid Poplar (*Populus deltoides x Populus nigra*), and Eastern Rosebud (*Cercis canadensis*).
What is the height and width of the trees?
Yellow Poplar Tuliptree—70' to 90' height with 40' spread
Hybrid Poplar—40' to 50' height with 30' spread
Eastern Rosebud—20' to 30' height with 30' spread

Sample 2—Supply List

Yellow Poplar Tuliptree

Hybrid Poplar Tree
Eastern Rosebud Tree
Shovel
Gloves

Sample 3—Tree-Planting Campaign

What area is in desperate need of trees? Neighborhood Park
What types of trees are needed? Trees that will provide lots of shade
Tree planting committee: Rebecca Lund

    Jessica Robertson

    Andy Ward

    Tina Arles

Kevin Janney
Tree store: Turners Greenland
Contact person: Arthur Cotton, Manager Phone number: 784-8174
Multiple tree discount: 10%
Tree order: American Holly (Ilex opaca) 40'–50' mature height
Soil type: The American Holly grows in acidic, drought tolerant, loamy, moist, rich, sandy, well-drained, wide range, clay soils
Sun: The American Holly does well in full sun, partial shade.
$9.00 per tree

Tree order: Red Maple (*Acer rubrum*) 40' –60' mature height
Soil Type: The Red Maple grows in acidic, loamy, moist, rich, sandy, silty loam, well-drained, wet, clay soils.
Sun: The red maple does well in full sun, partial shade.
$9.00 per tree

Tree order: Leyland Cypress (*X Cupressocyparis leylandii*) 60'–70' mature height
Soil type: The Leyland Cypress grows in acidic, alkaline, drought tolerant, loamy, moist, rich, sandy, well-drained, wide range, clay soils.
Sun: This Leyland Cypress does well in full sun.
$13.50 per tree

Tree order: Camellia (*Camellia sasanqua*) 6'-10' mature height
Soil type: The Camellia grows in acidic, loamy, moist, rich, sandy, silty loam,

well-drained soils.

Sun: The Camellia does well in full sun, partial shade.

$9.00 per tree

Campaign Note to Neighborhood Residents

Dear Resident,

Our neighborhood park is in desperate need of trees! A handful of neighborhood residents have formed a committee to organize a tree-planting project for our park. This project is very important not only to our environment but also for future generations of children who will be playing and enjoying this park. Please take time out of your busy schedule and help plant a tree. We will begin this very exciting project Saturday, March 25th at 9 a.m. Please e-mail Jasper Newman at Jasper.Newman@familyemailaddress.com to confirm your participation.

Thank you.

Any money donations are welcomed for the purchase of the trees.

Please send to: Jasper Newman, 601 Cottonwood, Kingsville, Texas 78363

Sample 4—Keeping Track

Donors	Address	Amount Donated
Jessica Robertson	601 Cottonwood	$10.00
Louis Caldwell	603 Cottonwood	$5.00
Nina Calderon	605 Cottonwood	$20.00
Tina Arles	607 Cottonwood	$25.00
William Sullivan	609 Cottonwood	$5.00
Michael Zach	611 Cottonwood	$15.00
Paola Gilberto	613 Cottonwood	$10.00
Maria Quintanilla	615 Cottonwood	$10.00
Rebecca Lund	617 Cottonwood	$15.00
Rachel Byrd	619 Cottonwood	$20.00
Shannon Millwee	211 Sagebrush	$20.00
Kevin Janney	213 Sagebrush	$10.00
Lynette Berry	215 Sagebrush	$5.00
Andy Ward	217 Sagebrush	$15.00
Iris Trejo	219 Sagebrush	$20.00
Richard Lavay	221 Sagebrush	$15.00
Chandra Young	223 Sagebrush	$10.00
Melissa Harris	225 Sagebrush	$20.00

Brian Watson	227 Sagebrush	$10.00
Emma Samson	229 Sagebrush	$15.00
Amanda Woods	231 Sagebrush	$10.00
Victor Deleon	233 Sagebrush	$20.00
Katie Marshall	405 Firewood	$50.00
Larry Hall	407 Firewood	$20.00
Orlando Billups	409 Firewood	$10.00
Patricia Plummer	411 Firewood	$15.00
Chris Hall	413 Firewood	$5.00
Devonte Hunter	415 Firewood	$20.00
Beatrice Atkins	417 Firewood	$50.00
Piper Tomlin	419 Firewood	$10.00
Nadia Ponte	421 Firewood	$15.00
Audrey Haynes	423 Firewood	$20.00
Pat Scheiner	425 Firewood	$15.00
Allen Bowen	427 Firewood	$20.00
William Hovanic	429 Firewood	$20.00
Bruce Marshall	431 Firewood	$10.00
Cameron Franco	433 Firewood	$5.00
Penelope Walsh	435 Firewood	$30.00
Pinky Garza	437 Firewood	$25.00
Tatum Melon	439 Firewood	$5.00
TOTAL:		$650.00

Tree Planters	Phone number	Address
Rebecca Lund	425-8756	617 Cottonwood
Jessica Robertson	425-7845	601 Cottonwood
Andy Ward	425-7006	217 Sagebrush
Tina Arles	425-7843	607 Cottonwood
Kevin Janney	425-0495	213 Sagebrush
Audrey Haynes	425-5778	423 Firewood
Devonte Hunter	425-8585	415 Firewood
Nina Calderon	425-1578	605 Cottonwood
Rachel Byrd	425-8204	619 Cottonwood
Emma Samson	425-1848	229 Sagebrush
Piper Tomlin	425-8493	419 Firewood
Bruce Marshall	425-7503	431 Firewood
Lynette Berry	425-8450	215 Sagebrush

Chandra Young   425-7892   223 Sagebrush
Amanda Woods   425-8532   231 Sagebrush
Nolan Newman (me)
Jasper Newman (Dad)

Sample 5—Thank-You Notes

Note to Tree Planters:

Chandra,

Thank you very much for participating with the neighborhood's park tree-planting project. It turned out to be a beautiful day filled with teamwork and helpfulness.

Thank you again,

Nolan Newman

Note to money donations:

Nina,

Thank you for the generous donation you gave toward the purchase of our neighborhood park's trees. Because of you, our whole neighborhood will be able to enjoy sitting under beautiful trees for years to come.

Nolan Newman

I'm not an environmentalist. I'm an Earth warrior.
—Darryl Cherney, Environmental Activist

Activity 6

Learn How to Make Compost

Compost is one of nature's best natural fertilizers. Composting also helps with recycling kitchen scraps. Plus you can make it without spending a cent.

Step 1

Compost begins with you.

To make compost, you must collect yard and kitchen wastes such as fallen leaves, grass clippings, weeds, remains of garden plants, vegetable and fruit scraps, coffee grounds and filters, tea bags, wood chips, straw, egg shells, and small twigs, to name a handful. Make a list of what you can and cannot use for your compost and post it on your refrigerator. See Sample 1.

Step 2

Why you should make compost.

Compost improves your soil and the plants growing in it. Organic matter in the soil improves plant growth by helping to break up heavy clay soils or adds water and holds nutrients for sandy soil. It also adds essential nutrients to all other soils. If you have a garden, a lawn, trees, shrubs, or even plant boxes, you have a use for compost.

Step 3

Build a compost holding unit.

Holding units are containers, bins, or structures for holding organic materials in place during the composting process. Portable units may be made from lightweight materials, such as wire mesh, chicken wire, and hardware cloth. Permanent units are made with heavier materials such as a wooden pallet or concrete blocks. There are also turning units that can be made to turn the compost easily. A nonbuilding way to go is using a metal garbage can, but a disadvantage of using a garbage can is that it's hard to turn the compost. Have your mom or dad get involved with your project. Speak to them about the location of your holding unit. Go to your local book store or library to research how to build your holding unit.

Step 4

Bake your compost.

After you've built your holding unit, you're ready to start baking your compost. To bake a quick batch of compost, start by putting the first layers of outdoor materials such as leaves and grass into your holding unit. Make sure you chop or spread the organic materials. Also, spread soil or already completed compost over the compost pile. This layer helps keep the surface from drying out. To adjust the moisture in your compost pile, add straw or sawdust to the soggy materials, or add water to the pile if it's too dry. The materials should be damp to the touch, but not so wet that drops come out when you squeeze it. Allow the pile to bake. It should heat quickly and reach the desire temperature of 90 140 degrees Fahrenheit in four to five days. Stir your compost as it bakes if you want to speed the process. If the compost is baking properly you will notice that the pile will settle down from its original height. If you mix or turn your compost pile every week, it should be ready in one to two months, and if you don't turn it the compost it will be ready in six to twelve months. When your compost is ready, it should look like a dark crumbly soil mixed with small pieces of organic material with a sweet earth smell. Use it to feed your plants, garden, trees, shrubs, or lawn by mixing it with the soil. However, don't use your compost to sprout new seeds. The fungus in the compost could kill the seed.

Step 5

Keep track.

Take notes of what you're adding to your compost and approximately how much. This will be useful to you as you've baked a few batches of compost. Also, keep track of how often you turn your compost. See Sample 2.

Step 6

Invite people over.

Show off your composting holding unit! You should be very proud of yourself and your family for their effort with recycling organic materials.

Step 7

Make compost recipe cards.

This is a great opportunity to spread awareness. Make and hand out recipe cards with compost ingredients listed. You can also add to your recipe cards what not to use for your compost. See Sample 3.

Step 8

Make a poster board or display board.

Show others how to make compost by posting it on an awareness board at school. Take pictures of your own compost process to show how its suppose to look..

Step 9

Keep a journal.

Write about your compost. Do you like making compost? Are you having fun? Does your yard look healthier after using your compost?

Step 10

Make people aware of composting.

Create a newsletter. Ask your local garden shop if you could place your newsletters in their store for customers to take with them.

Sample 1—Compost List

Use	*Don't Use*
Melon rinds	Meat
Carrot peelings	Bones
Tea bags	Cheese
Apple cores	Cat or dog droppings
Banana peels	Milk
Potato peels	High Fat Food
Egg shells	Oil
Grass clippings	Diseased Plants
Dried leaves	Peanut butter
Hay or straw	Ashes from coal or charcoal
Shredded cardboard	Fish scraps

Coffee ground and filters   Lime
Hair
Shredded b/w newspaper
Sawdust and wood shavings
Seaweed (Rinse off salt water)
Cornstalks or corn cobs
Dried out weeds
Dryer lint
Nutshells
Vegetable scraps

Sample 2—Keeping Track

Batch 1

Compost Materials Added	Compost Turned
Grass clippings	May 6
Raked leaves	May 13
Egg shells	May 20
Vegetables scraps	May 27
Corn cobs	June 3
Banana peels	June 10
Coffee grounds	June 17—Compost is Baked!
Hair	
Apple cores	

Batch 2

Compost Materials Added	Compost Turned
Grass clippings	May 20
Egg shells	May 27
Vegetable scraps	June 3
Watermelon rind	June 10
Shredded b/w newspaper	June 17
Dryer lint	June 24
Banana peels	July 1
Tea bags	July 7—Compost is Baked!
Wood shavings	
Nutshells	

Batch 3

Compost Materials Added	Compost Turned
Grass clippings	June 3
Vegetable scraps	June 10
Fruit scraps	June 17
Egg shells	June 24
Shredded cardboard	July 1
Hair	July 7
Potato peels	July 14
Nutshells	July 21—Compost is Baked!
Dryer lint	
Straw	

Sample 3—Compost Recipe Cards

Recipe: Compost _____From the kitchen of: Riley Hernandez_____
Mix the following household materials to a compost holding unit.

> melon rinds, carrot peelings, tea bags, apple cores, banana peels, potato peels, egg shells, grass clippings, dried leaves, hay or straw, shredded cardboard, shredded black/white newspaper, sawdust or wood shavings, seaweed (rinsed), cornstalks or corn cobs, dried out weeds, dryer lint, nutshells, and vegetable scraps

DO NOT USE THE FOLLOWING INGREDIENTS TO YOUR COMPOST:
bones, cheese, cat or dog droppings, milk, high fat foods, oil, diseased plants, peanut butter, ashes from coal or charcoal, fish scraps, and lime.

The ultimate camping trip was the Lewis and Clark expedition.
—Dave Barry

Activity 7

Host a Camping Trip

Make Others Aware of Camping Safety

This activity requires adult supervision at all times. If you're inviting a large group of friends, you'll need one chaperone for every three kids.

Step 1

Plan a safe camping trip.

Hosting a safe camping trip can be one of the most memorable experiences you will have. Knowing your limits, taking the time to plan ahead, and packing the right items will help your adventure go off without a hitch. Scout out the area you plan to camp at before your trip. You don't necessarily have to camp in the woods or forest, you can camp in your own backyard. Speak to your parents about this. See Sample 1.

Step 2

Plan ahead.

If you're not an experienced camper, begin your adventures by taking day trips to your camping location. However, even during day trips, you have to be aware of camping safety issues, such as insect bites and stings; plants that may cause rashes and allergic reactions; exposure to heat, wind, water, and cold; and getting lost.

Step 3

Supply list.

Make a supply list of the items you'll need for your host camping trip. Don't forget to give your invited guests a list of items they will need for the camping trip. See Sample 2.

Step 4

Where to pitch a tent?

Pitch your tent in a safe spot. Make sure your tent is made of a flame-retardant fabric, and set up far enough away from the campfire. Keep insects out of your tent by closing the entrance quickly when entering or leaving.

Step 5

Fire safety.

Make sure your campfire is always attended. Be sure you have chosen an area for your fire that cannot spread laterally or vertically— a grill or stone surface is ideal. When putting the fire out, drown it with water, making sure all embers, coals, and sticks are wet. Embers buried deep within the pile have a tendency to reignite later.

Step 6

Beware of wild animals and poisonous plants.

To ward off bears, keep your camp site clean, and do not leave food, garbage, coolers, cooking equipment, or utensils out in the open. Remember that bears are potentially dangerous and unpredictable—never feed or approach a bear. Use a flashlight at night— many animals feed at night, and the use of a flashlight may warn them away. Also, familiarize yourself with any dangerous plants that are common to the area. If you come into contact with a poisonous plant, immediately rinse the affected area with water and apply a soothing lotion such as calamine to the affected area.

Step 7

Practice good hygiene.

Make sure you wash your hands, particularly after using the toilet and before handling food, to prevent everyone in your group becoming ill. If your campsite doesn't have restrooms, you'll need to dig a hole and then cover it back up with dirt once you've finished your business. Also, remember to use biodegradable toilet paper.

Step 8

Have fun.

While you're camping with your friends, sing campfire songs or roast marshmallows to make S'mores. If you have a particular agenda for your campfire experience, be prepared for your activities and don't forget to take lots of pictures! See Sample 3.

Step 9

Clean up!

Dispose of trash properly. Remember to recycle—use the proper recycling bins if available.

Step 10

Thank your friends, chaperones, and parents.

Remember to send your thank-you notes. Let your friends know how much fun you had camping with them. Also, thank your parents and chaperones for helping you make the entire camping trip lots of fun and safe. See Sample 4.

Sample 1—Record Keeping

Where are you camping? Beaver Trail Campground
Location: 4408 Grass Lake Rd., West Branch, MI 48661
Web site: www.beavertrailcampground.com
What days will you camp? May 24th—May 27th
What are the daily rates? $25.00 per day
What does the campsite have to offer? Modern shower house, dump station, horseshoes, playground, and small private lake
How many friends are you going to invite? 6

Sample 2- Supply List

Tent
Sleeping bag/pillow
First aid kit
A map
Compass
Flashlight
Knife
Warm clothing
Food/storage for food so that animals can't smell it
Water

Insect protection
Calamine lotion
Sun screen
Warm clothes
Matches
Toilet paper
Plate/utensils
Food

Sample 3—Entertaining Plan

Making S'mores

Here's what you'll need:
Hershey's plain chocolate
Marshmallows
Graham crackers

Sing songs

Here's what you'll need:
Copies of Campfire Songs
Some suggested songs
> *Kumbaya*
> *Home on the Range*
> *Oh Susanna!*
> *On Top of Old Smoky*
> *This Land is Your Land*
> *Down in the Valley*

Tell Spooky Campfire Stories

Here's what you'll need:
Flashlight to light up your face
The book: *Scary Story Reader (American Storytelling)*, by Richard Young
Here are some of the story titles included in the book:
"Hook Arm," "Don't look back," "The call from the Grave," and "The White Dress."
Memorize them before your camping trip.

Scavenger Hunt

Here's what you'll need:

Copy of scavenger hunt list for each team

>Scavenger Hunt List
>Acorn
>Animal tracks
>Feather
>Flower
>Insect
>Different leaves
>Rocks
>Pine cones
>Sand
>Branch
>Piece of litter left behind by someone
>Snail
>Worm
>Pine needles

Finish the Story

Here's what you'll need:

A great imagination

Here's how it's played: One person begins a story with a couple of sentences and the next person adds on.

Sample 4—Thank-You Note

Dear Carson,

I just wanted to let know that I had so much fun on our camping trip. Your skylight tent was the perfect place to tell our spooky stories. I hope we can all do it next year.

Your friend,

Shay

Plants give us oxygen for the lungs and for the soul.—Linda Solegato, Author

Activity 8

Volunteer at a Greenhouse or Nursery

Greenhouses provide several types of advantages. Agriculturally, green-houses help produce healthy seedlings of varieties that can grow before spring planting, including heirloom and hard-to-find crops. Greenhouses also provide important educational space to teach service learning groups and individuals before field planting season begins.

Step 1

Make contact.

Introduce yourself. Find out if there is a training period at your local greenhouse. Let the person in charge know why you want to volunteer. See Sample 1.

Step 2

Educate yourself.

Learn all you can about soil, seeds, and plants.

Step 3

Commit yourself.

Give yourself a start date and an end date. Decide to volunteer for at least six months to a year, twice a week. Your commitment will be a valuable asset to yourself and to others. See Sample 2.

Step 4

Duties, responsibilities, requirements, and expectations.

Remember to follow directions for the duties that are required of you. Be respectful and responsible and know what is expected of your task.

Step 5

Execute a project.

Ask if you could start a rose garden or plant tree seedlings, timing it right, to begin once your native tree potting assignment has been completed.

Step 6

Nurture your project.

Give your project the attention it deserves. Water your seedlings and talk to them.

Step 7

Watch it grow!

Keep track of the progression of its growth. Use markers to remind yourself of your seedlings or plants. Continue to check up on your planted seedlings even after you volunteer commitment has ended. See Sample 3.

Step 8

Keep a journal.

What did you like most about volunteering at the greenhouse? Did you make any new friends? Write down all your thoughts and feelings about your new experiences at the greenhouse.

Step 9

Display board.

Make a Display board with pictures of your experiences at the greenhouse. Be creative and have fun!

Step 10

Promote the greenhouse.

Encourage everyone you know to visit the greenhouse to look at all the beautiful flowers and trees. Also, ask people to donate any funds they can to support the greenhouse.

Sample 1—Record Keeping

Name of Greenhouse: King County Greenhouse
Spoke with: Wayne Carver Date: January 31st
Phone number: 524-4795 Contact time: 3:30 p.m.
E-mail: Wayne.Carver@KingCountyGreenHouse.Com
Volunteer position available: To help pot seedlings of native trees and

shrubs at the King County Greenhouse.

Sample 2—Volunteer Schedule

Start Date: March 4, 2007 End Date: September 4, 2007
March
Saturday
3 Native Tree Potting 9:00—1:00
10 Native Tree Potting 9:00—1:00
17 Native Tree Potting 9:00—1:00
24 Native Tree Potting 9:00 -1:00
31 Native Tree Potting 9:00—1:00
April
Saturday
7 Native Tree Potting 9:00—1:00
14 Native Tree Potting 9:00—1:00
21 Native Tree Potting 9:00—1:00
28 Native Tree Potting 9:00—1:00
May
Saturday
5 Native Tree Potting 9:00—1:00
12 Native Tree Potting 9:00—1:00
19 Native Tree Potting 9:00—1:00
26 Native Tree Potting 9:00—1:00
June
Saturday
3 Native Tree Potting 9:00—1:00
10 Native Tree Potting 9:00—1:00
17 Seedling Planting 9:00—1:00
24 Seedling Planting 9:00—1:00
July
Saturday
1 Family Trip
8 Family Trip
15 Family Trip
22 Volunteer Support 9:00—1:00
29 Volunteer Support 9:00—1:00
August

Saturday

5 Volunteer Support 9:00—1:00

12 Volunteer Support 9:00—1:00

19 Volunteer Support 9:00—1:00

26 Volunteer Support 9:00—1:00

September

Saturday

2 Family Trip

9 Last Day—Volunteer Support 9:00—1:00

Sample 3—Keeping Track

Project: Planting Bigleaf Maple seedling

How many seedlings did you plant? 10

Bigleaf Maple seedling's growth chart

Seed	Growth	Date	Growth	Date	Growth	Date	Growth	Date
#1	0.5cm	Jul 22	.75cm	Jul 29	1cm	Aug 5	1.25cm	Aug 12
#2	1cm	Jul 22	1.25cm	Jul 29	1.5cm	Aug 5	2cm	Aug 12
#3	0.5cm	Jul 22	.5 cm	Jul 29	1cm	Aug 5	1.75cm	Aug 12
#4	1.5cm	Jul 22	1.75cm	Jul 29	2cm	Aug 5	2.25cm	Aug 12
#5	1cm	Jul 22	1cm	Jul 29	1.25cm	Aug 5	1.5cm	Aug 12
#6	0.5cm	Jul 22	.75cm	Jul 29	1cm	Aug 5	1cm	Aug 12
#7	1.5cm	Jul 22	2cm	Jul 29	2.25cm	Aug 5	2.5cm	Aug 12
#8	1.5cm	Jul 22	2cm	Jul 29	2cm	Aug 5	2.75cm	Aug 12
#9	1cm	Jul 22	1.5cm	Jul 29	1.75cm	Aug 5	2.25cm	Aug 12
#10	None	Jul 22	None	Jul 29	.25cm	Aug 5	.5cm	Aug 12

If you play with fire, you're gonna get burned.—Saying

Activity 9

Promote Fire Safety

This activity is very important. Everyone needs to know the dangers of fires and hazardous consumer products in your home.

Step 1

Educate yourself.

Fires are very dangerous. They hurt and destroy things in your home. Learn all there is to know about fire safety so that you can become an expert.

Step 2

Begin at home.

Go through your home, with your parents. Prepare a list of fire safety precautions and safety supplies. Also, keep track of your fire alarm detector checks. See Sample 1.

Step 3

Fire drill.

What would you do if there were a fire in your home? It's important to get out fast! Never hide or take time to gather your belongings. The best plans have two ways to get out of each room. If one way is blocked by fire, you can use the other way. Have fire drills with your family. Draw a plan of your home with arrows pointing toward the *safest escape route possible.* See Sample 2.

Step 4

What starts fires?

Make a list of items that could potentially become a fire hazard. See Sample 3.

Step 5

Guest speaker.

Invite a firefighter to your school or neighborhood to discuss the importance of fire safety. If you plan your promotion for fire safety at school, be sure to check with your principal. Or send invitations to your neighbors if your guest will be speaking to your neighborhood block. See Sample 4.

Step 6

Make fire safety badges.

Design a fire safety badge for your fellow classmates and or neighbors. Pass out questionnaires with true/false questions so that classmates or neighbors can quiz themselves. See Sample 5.

Step 7

Pass out fire safety material.

Make brochures with facts about fire safety and pass them out! See Sample 6.

Step 8

Make a display board.

Find a location for your display board. Add important information. Be creative and have fun.

Step 9

Keep a journal.

Write your thoughts and feelings about your experiences about fire safety. Did you learn a lot about your family fire drill? Were there fire hazards in your home?

Step 10

Spread the awareness.

Tell everyone what you've learned about fire safety. Promote the importance of smoke alarms and fire drills at home.

Sample 1—Fire Precautions and Safety Supplies

Fire Precautions

1. Never put anything over a lamp, like clothes or a blanket, not even when you are playing.

2. Don't touch radiators or heaters. Ask an adult to turn a heater on or off for you.

3. Don't stand too close to the fireplace or a wood stove. You could get burned or your clothes could catch fire. Also, fireplaces should have screens.

4. Never touch matches, lighters, or candles. If you see matches or lighters in a room, tell an adult right away.

5. Don't cook alone or without asking an adult. Remind your parents to turn pot handles toward the center of the stove.

Safety Supplies

Smoke alarms

Monthly checks on smoke alarms

Know what smoke alarms sound like

Replace old batteries with brand new ones at least once a year

Keep smoke alarms clean from dust

Fire extinguisher

Monthly checks on all fire extinguishers

Make sure the extinguisher is stored in a proper location.

The whole family should know where to find each fire extinguisher.

The operating tag of the extinguisher should always be facing out.

The tamper seal of the extinguisher should always be intact.

Feel the weight of the fire extinguisher, it should feel full.

The shell of the extinguisher should be in good condition.

The fire extinguisher should have a hazardous material identification system label on the canister.

The discharge nozzle should be free of clogging.

Keeping Track—Fire Alarm Detector Checks

Jan. 1, 2007—Passed	Jul. 1, 2007—Dusted/passed
Feb. 1, 2007—Passed	Aug. 1, 2007—Replaced kitchen fire alarm
Mar. 1, 2007—Dusted/Passed	Sep. 1, 2007—Passed
Apr. 1, 2007—Passed	Oct. 1, 2007—Passed
May 1, 2007—Changed batteries	Nov. 1, 2007—Dusted/passed
Jun. 1, 2007—Passed	Dec. 1, 2007—Passed

Sample 2—Fire Escape Plan & Information

When escaping stay low to the floor. Smoke rises during a fire. The safest air is down low.

Try to find two ways out from every room in your home. The first way out should be a door. Every way needs to be planned, and practice your escape with grown-ups.

Before opening any door in a fire, feel the door first at the bottom and then work your hand up the door to see if it is hot. A hot door means there may be fire on the other side. Try to get out another way.

If you have security bars on your windows, make sure you know how to open them in case you need to escape from a fire.

If you live in a two-story house, purchase a two-story fire escape ladder that you can hang from your window to climb out just in case you can't escape from your bedroom door.

Pick a safe and easy-to-remember place outside the home to meet your family after you get out.

After you get out call 9-1-1 or the fire department.

Stay outside no matter what. Don't go back for anything. Nothing is worth more than your life.

Sample 3—Fire Hazard Checklist

Checklist of Items that could be a Fire Hazard
Candles
Clothes dryer—If you do not clean the filter.
Matches
Battery packs
Cooking over a stove with long sleeves that hang over
Outlets
Propane tank
Gasoline can
Unattended iron
Unattended coffee maker
Unattended stove
Unattended space heater

Sample 4—Guest Speaker

Name of guest speaker: Captain Ronald Trevino
Contact e-mail address: CaptainRonaldTrevino@emailaddress.com

Contact phone number: 758-7403
Principal's name: Betty Shands
Contact phone number: 758-4274
School's name: Westbrook Elementary School
Location of speaking event: Westbrook Elementary School's Cafeteria
Time of speaking event: 10:00 a.m.–11:30 a.m.
Special instructions: Please make sure no one's parked in the front parking lot. Captain Trevino will be bringing a fire truck so that all the students can tour the truck and hear the sirens.

Sample 5—True/False Questionnaire

What do you know about fire safety?

Smoke alarms make a loud ringing noise. T or F
Smoke alarms should be tested once a month. T or F
Smoke alarms should hang on your wall. T or F
You should stay low to the ground when escaping a fire. T or F
You should never go back into a burning building for something you treasure. T or F
You should have a safe and easy-to-remember place to meet your family after you get out. T or F
You should pack all your toys up before escaping a fire. T or F
You should have two escape routes from every room in your home. T or F
You should plan a fire drill with your family. T or F
After you go outside, you should call your friends. T or F

Correct Answers:
  F beeping noises
  T
  F hang on your ceiling
  T
  T
  T
  F you should never try to pack anything. Get out and leave everything behind! Nothing is more important than your life.
  T
  T
  F You need to call 9-1-1

Every day is Earth Day.—Author Unknown

Activity 10

Celebrate Earth Day and Everyday

If you've completed any or all of the last nine environmental awareness activities, you're celebrating our earth on a daily basis. Thank you for caring for our planet earth.

Step 1

Learn the history.

Earth Day is celebrated every year on April 22. Learn why and when Earth Day began.

Step 2

Prepare and propose a week-long of activities celebrating our earth.

One week before Earth Day, fill your week with daily activities. Propose this plan to your principal well in advance or plan to do this with your family at home. Post flyers at school one week before the week-long celebrations begin, listing each day's activity. See Sample 1.

Step 3

Day 1 Activity—Earth Day Reading Skit.

Write a skit about the origin of Earth Day. Read your skit over the school intercom with a friend or classmate during your school's morning announcements. Have your principal announce the beginning of your week-long celebration. See Sample 2.

Step 4

Day 2 Activity—Guest Speaker.

Invite your local city's environmental manager to your school to speak about Earth Day. As soon as you receive approval from your principal, contact the office of your city environmental manager. Even if it's five months in advance, it's very important that you have a guest speaker locked in for the event. See Sample 3.

Step 5

Day 3 Activity—Litterless Lunch.

Work with your school cafeteria to plan on meals that require little or no garbage. Write down what you usually have on your lunch tray. See Sample 4.

Step 6

Day 4 Activity—Wear Green.

Have a green clothing day to show your support of the earth. Encourage everyone to wear green.

Step 7

Day 5 Activity—Pledge Card.

During Earth Week, make a pledge to do your part, all year, to help keep the planet healthy. Whether it's reducing the amount of garbage you make, recycling your trash, or just buying less stuff, you can make a difference! Make pledge cards for everyone at school.

Step 8

Day 6 Activity—Plant a tree.

What a wonderful tradition you can start at school. Speak to your principal about planting a tree each year to celebrate Earth Day.

Step 9

Day 7 Activity—Earth Day Celebration.

Make a round cake, in the shape of our earth, for your class to eat at the end of the school day. Encourage all the other classrooms to make cakes for their class. Perhaps you could ask your PTA to make round cakes for each classroom.

Step 10

Make a display board.

Post photographs of your week-long activities celebrating Earth Day on a display board for your whole school to see. Have fun. Ask others to help you with your display board.

Sample 1—Earth Day Week-Long Daily Activities

Earth Day Celebration Week
Monday, April 19th—Friday, April 23

Monday—Earth Day Reading Skit (Morning Announcements)
Tuesday—Guest Speaker (Gym @ 11:00)
Wednesday—Litterless Lunch
Thursday—Wear Green, Today is Earth Day!
Friday—Sign your Pledge Card, and Make Every Day Earth Day
Thank You for your Participation!

Sample 2—Earth Day Skit

To be read during the morning announcements, Monday, April 19th.

> Stella: Hi Nina.
> Nina: Hi Stella.
> Stella: What are you reading?
> Nina: Oh I'm reading all about Earth Day.
> Stella: Earth Day?
> Nina: Yes, Earth Day. Earth Day is celebrated every year on April 22nd.
> Stella: What do you do on Earth Day?
> Nina: Well, it's a day when everyone should act and promote awareness of environmental issues such as recycling, conserving energy, and water and driving less.
> Stella: Shouldn't we do that everyday?
> Nina: Of course we should! But I think if people aren't aware of what they should do, Earth Day is a good start to make others aware of what they can do.
> Stella: Well hopefully we can all learn and cherish the earth by participating in recycling, conserving energy and water, and driving less and walking more.
> Nina: I hope so because if we don't take care of our earth, we can never go back and correct the damage that's already done. It takes everyone's participation.
> Stella: Thanks Nina for explaining Earth Day to me. You can count on me to cherish our earth.

Sample 3—Record Keeping—Guest Speaker

Name of speaker: Mrs. June Rose, City Environmental Manager

1st contact date: November 2nd   1st contact time: 9:30 a.m.

2nd contact date: April 5th   2nd contact time: 10:45 a.m.

Phone number: 763-6722

E-mail: June.Rose@EnvironmentalOffice.com

Date requesting speaker: Tuesday, April 20th

Time: 11:00 a.m.–11:45 a.m.

Sample 4—Litterless Lunch Plan

Cafeteria Manager: Ms. Kimberly Stewart

Date planned for Litterless Lunch: Wednesday, April 21st

Menu Planned: Pepperoni pizza

    Carton chocolate milk

    Carrots

    Pineapple

    Vanilla custard

SECTION FIVE

Animal Husbandry

Animals are such agreeable friends, they ask no questions, they pass no criticisms.—George Eliot

A dog wags its tail with its heart.—Martin Buxbaum, former Director of Communications of the Marriott Corporation

Activity 1

Volunteer at your Local Animal Shelter

Working with animals is one of the most rewarding experiences you'll ever have. It will also make life brighter for the pets in our care, and better for the people and animals in our community.

Step 1

Locate an animal shelter.

Look in your phone book for a listing of animal shelters. Animal shelters are called different names, so look in the Yellow Pages under listings such as "animal shelter," "humane society," or "animal control." Public animal care and control agencies are often listed under the city or county health department or police department. Speak to the volunteer coordinator or the manager of the animal shelter. Express your desire to volunteer at the animal shelter. Let him or her know why you want to help. Find out if there are any qualifications that you'll have to meet to volunteer at the shelter. See Sample 1.

Step 2

Lend a hand.

Bathe and groom the animals, walk dogs, or play with cats. Clean animal cages, change food and water, stuff envelopes for mass mailings, or help publicize an event. Ask what your responsibilities are at the animal shelter. Express what you're good at doing and what you would like to do.

Step 3

Be committed.

Speak to your parent(s) about how often you can spend volunteering at the animal shelter. Give the shelter the days and time you wish to volunteer. Stick to your schedule, once you sign up to volunteer, the animal shelter depends on you to be there for them and for the animals. See Sample 2.

Step 4

Be a hero.

Report animal cruelty and neglect as well as injured or stray animals. You may prevent suffering and even save a life. You can contact your local humane society, animal shelter, or animal control agency immediately. In most areas, these agencies have the authority to enforce state and local laws related to animals and have the capability to investigate and resolve these situations. They rely on concerned citizens to be their eyes and ears in the community and to report animal suffering. You can choose to remain anonymous, although giving your name to your humane agency will enable that group to follow up with you when necessary.

Step 5

Make a donation.

Most animal shelters will accept donations such as dog or cat food, old blankets and towels, or other needed supplies. Make others aware of these supplies that are generally needed.

Step 6

Contact the media.

Ask your local newspaper and television station to write or tape a special report about your local animal shelter. Have them express the need for adoption to good homes for these animals and the vast growing problem of homeless domestic pets.

Step 7

Make a display board.

Display your display board at your school, at a local college, or at a local pet store. Give important information about the animal shelter. Post pictures of some of the animals that are waiting for adoption. Give it your all because your display board could change an animal's life forever.

Step 8

Keep a journal.

Express your feelings and experiences in your journal. Explain how the animal shelter has made an impact on you. Did you make an impact? What did you learn? Is there anything that you would like to change?

Step 9

Help spread the word.

Tell your friends and family about the animal shelter. Encourage them to visit the animal shelter and the programs it has to offer.

Step 10

Hand out "Thank-You" notes.

Thank the employees, at the animal shelter, for showing you around the shelter and helping you with various jobs. Don't forget to thank your parents for their support and for driving you to and from the animal shelter. See Sample 3.

Sample 1—Record Keeping

Name of Animal Shelter: North Shore Animal League America
Spoke with: Jane Pepper   Date: August 4th
Phone number: 883-7575 Contact time: 11:00 a.m.
E-mail: hr@nsalamerica.org
Mailing address: 25 Davis Avenue, Port Washington, NY 11050
Qualifications Required? Fill out Volunteer Form (Application)
Volunteer Position Available:
Cat Habitat Volunteer_____
Requirements: Must be a mature individual and able to work very independently.
Hours Needed: Various Hours, Mon through Sun (several positions available)__
Responsibilities: Cleaning & handling cats and kittens in habitat, providing information to adopters, filling out applications.
Commitment: 6 months—Year   Hours: 3-hour shifts

Sample 2—Volunteer Schedule

August

Sun	Mon	Tues	Wed	Thurs	Fri	Sat
1	2	3	4	5	6	7
	3-6		3-6		3-6	9-12
8	9	10	11	12	13	14
	3-6		3-6		3-6	9-12

15	16	17	18	19	20	21
	3-6		3-6		3-6	9-12
22	23	24	25	26	27	28
	3-6		3-6		3-6	9-12
29	30					
	3-6					

Sample 3—Thank-You Note

To the Staff at North Shore Animal League America,

I wanted to thank you so much for all the support and knowledge you gave to me. I learned what it takes to care for animals and how it's important that as a society we need to care for them. I plan to make it my life's mission to help animals.

Your friend,

Georgia Palmer

An animal's eyes have the power to speak a great language.—Martin Buber

Activity 2

Promote the Importance of Having Your Pets Spayed or Neutered

Having animals spayed or neutered can bring substantial rewards. Not only does it prevent overpopulation and abuse or neglect of unwanted animals, but it also will help animals live a healthier longer life.

Step 1

Make contact.

Call your local animal shelter or veterinarian. Ask about spay and neuter services. Find out how much it costs for cats and dogs to have the surgical procedure. Let them know that you want to encourage people to have their pets spayed or neutered. Find out if they would be willing to lower their costs for one week? See Sample 1.

Step 2

Learn about spay and neuter.

Educate yourself about the procedure and why it's important to have your pets spayed and neutered.

Step 3

Make an information sheet.

Look at all the positive aspects of having your pets spayed or neutered; add it to your information sheet. Once you've completed your information sheet, make copies of it and pass them out to people. See Sample 2.

Step 4

Organize an event.

Speak to the veterinarian or animal shelter about a promotional event for having pets spayed or neutered.

Step 5

Advertise your event.

Contact your local newspaper. Ask them to write about the importance of having your pet spayed or neutered and to mention your event. Give them important information. Tell them that it's a big possibility that your community is spending millions of dollars to control unwanted animals. See Sample 3.

Step 6

Be innovative.

Think of an incentive, with the approval of the clinic or animal shelter, for people to bring in their pets to be spayed or neutered. Maybe make the first 10 appointments free of charge for the procedure. Or hand out to all your pet parents goody bags with flea and tick prevention oil, dog shampoo, gourmet dog or cat food, chew treats, catnip, and a brush provided by a pet store. You'll need to request these items for donation from the pet store manager in advance.

Step 7

Help schedule appointments.

Become an active volunteer. Help the staff schedule the appointments. Learn what questions you'll need to ask each pet parent. Have a cheat sheet handy when you are scheduling the appointments.

Step 8

Make poster boards.

It's time to be creative! Post important information about having cats and dogs spayed or neutered. Hang the posters at various locations.

Step 9

Spread the awareness.

Spread the importance of having your pets spayed or neutered. Tell people that spaying and neutering helps dogs and cats live longer, healthier lives not to mention that spaying and neutering prevents the overabundance of unwanted animals.

Step 10

Thank the staff.

Express your gratitude for helping you with a successful event! See Sample 4.

Sample 1—Record Keeping

Veterinarian clinic: Buena Pet Clinic

Spoke with: Arthur Barrett, DVM   Date: March 18th

Phone number: 323-9487 Contact time: 2:45 p.m.

Mailing address: 6843 Ellis Road, Tucson AZ 85701

Regular cost for spaying: Cat $65.00

Dog 0-35lb. $75.00

31-60lb. $85.00

61-80lb. $95.00

81-100lb. $105.00

Regular cost for neutering: Cat $35.00

Special cost for one week of spaying and neutering pets: $25.00 for spay or neutered services for cats and dogs, despite weight for dogs.

Week of: Monday, June 6—Saturday, June 11

How many pets per day can have the procedure? 8

Appointments

Mon., June 6:

    8 a.m.—Mittens;

    9 a.m.—Boomer;

    10 a.m.—Tiger;

    11 a.m.—Suzy;

    12 p.m.—Lunch;

    1 p.m.—Casey;

    2 p.m.—Lulu;

    3 p.m.—Doogie;

    4 p.m.—Kiki

Tues., June 7:

    8 a.m.—Blue;

    9 a.m.—Caleb;

    10 a.m.—Swartz.

    11 a.m.—Maxwell

    12 p.m.—Lunch;

    1 p.m.—Mitsey;

    2 p.m.—Mimi;

    3 p.m.—Violet;

    4 p.m.—Baby

Wed., June 9:

    8 a.m.—Trevor;

    9 a.m.—Abbey;

    10 a.m.—Sam;

    11 a.m.—Pepe;

    12 p.m.—Lunch;

    1 p.m.—Honey;

    2 p.m.—Ginger;

    3 p.m.—Toby;

    4 p.m.—Mattie

Sample 2—Information Sheet

Spaying or Neutering is Good for Your Pet

Spaying and neutering helps dogs and cats live longer, healthier lives.

Spaying and neutering can eliminate or reduce the incidence of a number of health problems that can be very difficult or expensive to treat.

Spaying eliminates the possibility of uterine or ovarian cancer and greatly reduces the incidence of breast cancer, particularly when your pet is spayed before her first estrous cycle.

Neutering eliminates testicular cancer and decreases the incidence of prostate disease.

Spaying or neutering is good for you.

Spaying and neutering makes pets better, more affectionate companions.

Neutering cats makes them less likely to spray and mark territory.

Spaying a dog or cat eliminates her heat cycle. Estrus lasts an average of 6 to 12 days, often twice a year, in dogs, and an average of 6 to 7 days, three or more times a year, in cats. Females in heat can cry incessantly, show nervous behavior, and attract unwanted male animals.

Unsterilized animals often exhibit more behavior and temperament problems than do those who have been spayed or neutered.

Spaying and neutering can make pets less likely to bite.

Neutering makes pets less likely to roam the neighborhood, run away, or get into fights.

Spaying and Neutering are good for the community.

Communities spend millions of dollars to control unwanted animals.

Irresponsible breeding contributes to the problem of dog bites and attacks.

Animal shelters are overburdened with lots of animals.

Stray pets and homeless animals get into trash containers, defecate in public areas or on private lawns, and frighten or anger people who have no understanding of their misery or needs.

Some stray animals also scare away or kill birds and wildlife.

Sample 3—Newspaper Advertisement

Animal clinic provides low cost spaying and neutering. We know that spaying and neutering our pets is the best way to stop overpopulation, but the cost of this procedure is too expensive to many low-income pet parents. For one week, Buena Pet Clinic, will lower their spay and neutering service to the first 48 pet owners. Please call the clinic at 323-9487 for an appointment.

Sample 4—Thank-You Note

Dr. Barrett,

I would like to thank you for your kind and generous service. Lowering your cost for spaying and neutering cats and dogs has helped so many to be able to afford the procedure. I hope we can work together again.

Sincerely,

Robert Dahl

I like pigs. Dogs look up to us. Cats look down on us.
Pigs treat us as equals.—Winston Churchill

Activity 3

Volunteer at a Local Animal Farm

Animal farms can consist of different kinds of animals. We often think of farms as only having cows, horses, and pigs. Did you know that animal farms can also be refuges? Dogs that have been forced to fight with other dogs can live there. It can also be a rescue sanctuary for roosters, rabbits, goats, and all other kinds of animals. Choose one for which you'd like to volunteer.

Step 1

Make contact.

Find a local animal farm in your area. Introduce yourself and express the reasons why you would like to volunteer at their farm. Ask the director or owner of the farm what kinds of animals they care for. What kind of volunteer work is offered? Be prepared to ask and answer all questions given and received. See Sample 1.

Step 2

What do you have to offer?

Consider your skills. Are you a good painter? Maybe they have a barn to paint. Do you like to build things? You can probably help mend fences or build them all the way. Make a list of what you'd like to do while you're volunteering at the farm. See Sample 2.

Step 3

Be committed.

Remember, once you begin volunteering at the farm, the staff and animals are counting on you to be there. Make a time frame of how long you'd like to commit yourself for. Speak to your parents about what would be best for you and your family. Consider transportation to and from the farm. Keep a calendar of the time and days and months you plan on volunteering. See Sample 3.

Step 4

Make a wish list.

There are many things that are needed for the animals at the farm. Ask the director of the farm what items you can add to your list to recruit new sponsors to donate these materials. You can also add a note at the bottom of your wish list that any donation made is tax deductible. See Sample 4.

Step 5

Get sponsorship.

Start your recruiting with asking your family and neighbors first. Ask the big corporations, such as Home Depot, Wal-Mart, or Sam's Club if they would be willing to donate any of the materials on your list. See Sample 5.

Step 6

Keeping track.

Remember to keep track of those who have donated to the farm. See Sample 6.

Step 7

Keep a volunteer journal.

Did you make friends at the farm? What did you learn? Was it hard work? Write down all your experiences while volunteering at the farm. You'll love reading it later to remember how you felt and what you did on the farm.

Step 8

Make a poster board.

Show your friends and family your experiences on the farm through your poster board appearance. Take pictures while you're on the farm to add them to your poster board.

Step 9

Spread the word.

Tell everyone about the farm that you volunteer with! Ask your friends if they would like to volunteer too.

Step 10

Be thankful.

Remember to thank the farm staff for teaching you about the various volunteer opportunities you've learned about at the farm. Thank your parents for driving you to and from the farm. And last, thank the sponsors who've donated materials from the wish list. See Sample 7.

Sample 1—Record Keeping

Farm name: Sing Farm and Rescue Animal Sanctuary
Spoke with: Danny Petty   Date: May 6th
Phone number: 438-5872 Contact time: 12:30 p.m.
Mailing address: 647 Riley Road, Big Springs, Nebraska 69122
Types of animals on the farm: Horses, pigs, chickens, goats, sheep, turkeys, emus, and llamas_____
Kind of volunteer opportunities offered:
Weekday Helper—Feed, water, clean up, and give love to the animals. Must be responsible.
Fund-raising coordinator—Organize upcoming events, work with local businesses and other organizations. Must be enthusiastic, organized, and committed.
Volunteer schedule: May—October (6 months)/Twice a Week
Training Recommendations: None required

Sample 2—List of my Skills and Talents

Task oriented
Great with animals
Innovative
Friendly
Work great with others
Good organization skills

Sample 3—Volunteer Calendar

June

Sun	Mon	Tues	Wed	Thurs	Fri	Sat
1	2	3	4	5	6	7
						8-12

8	9	10	11	12	13	14
12-4						8-12
15	16	17	18	19	20	21
12-4						8-12
22	23	24	25	26	27	28
12-4						8-12
29	30					
12-4						

Sample 4—Wish List

There are many things that are needed for the animals at the farm, and remember, any donation is tax deductible.

Pickup truck that will pull 14' stock trailer

Tractor for moving things and digging trenches

Financial donations

Good goat hay.

Clean fresh straw for bedding for rabbits and pigs (in bales)

Corral panels

A good computer

File cabinet, in fairly good condition

Stall mats (if used, in good condition) for 12 x 12 horse stall, and various pig houses to keep dust down

Blankets for pigs

New or used—working water hoses

Horse fencing materials. Some of our fences are getting pretty run down.

Insulation for winterizing emu barns and pig houses

Pillow cases to make pillows for the pigs (they will be stuffed with the wool from the sheep)

Kid's plastic swimming pools (smallest) for the ducks and pigs. The ducks love to swim, and the pigs need to cool off in the summer as they are prone to heat stroke.

Also needed are:

Volunteers who can build awnings (for shade) onto current pig houses

Volunteers who can weatherproof current pig house

Volunteers that can contact hospitals for old blankets

Volunteers that can pick up loads of hay or straw

Volunteer administrative assistant, animal handler

Sample 5—List of Sponsorship

Sam's Club
Naylors Farm & Ranch Supply
Kay's Feed & Supply
Tomlinson's Feed & Pet Supplies
Costco
Invisible Fence Brand
Buck Moore Feed
Wal-Mart
Sears Roebuck & Co.

Sample 6—Keeping Track

Business	Items Donated	Receipt Given	Thank-You Sent
Samís Club	File cabinet	✓	✓
Nolanís Farm & Ranch Supply	Straw	✓	✓
Kayís Feed & Supply	Goat hay	✓	✓
Tomlinsonís Feed & Pet Supplies	Goat Hay	✓	✓
Costco	(5) Blankets / (3) Plastic swimming pools / (5) Entrance mats	✓	✓
Invisible Fence Brand	15' x 60' fence material for horse corral	✓	✓
Wal-Mart	(5) Water hoses / (4) Blankets / (10) Towels / (10) Pillow cases	✓	✓
Sears Roebuck & Co.	Refurbished tractor	✓	✓
Builders Square	Insulation	✓	✓

Sample 7—Thank-You Note

To the Staff and Management of Sears Lawn and Garden Department,
Thank you so much for the refurbished tractor! Your donation will help so
many volunteers and animals at the Sing Farm and Rescue Animal
Sanctuary.

Reagan Canter

A bird does not sing because it has an answer. It sings
because it has a song.—Chinese Proverb

Activity 4

Help Improve Your Local Bird Sanctuary

Bird sanctuaries are very important especially for threatened bird species.

Step 1

Make contact.

Locate your local bird sanctuary. Introduce yourself and express why you want to volunteer at the bird sanctuary. Ask the volunteer director what kinds of volunteer opportunities are offered. See Sample 1.

Step 2

What do you have to offer?

Make a list of what you have to offer the bird sanctuary. See Sample 2.

Step 3

Be committed.

Decide how long, what days, and the amount of hours you plan on volunteering your time to the bird sanctuary. Once you've committed yourself, be sure to be on time and ready to give it your all! There's a lot to learn and many birds to help.

Step 4

Educate yourself.

Learn about the history of the bird sanctuary. Also, educate yourself about the birds that live there.

Step 5

Plan an event.

Plan your event at the bird sanctuary celebrating its beautification. Serve slices of apple pie and tea. Send invitations to current members advertising your event. Encourage members to bring a guest with them. This could help to build the bird sanctuary's membership and spread awareness about the bird sanctuary. See Sample 3.

Step 6

Be innovative!

Think of something your bird sanctuary doesn't already have. Here are some ideas: draw a map of all the trails for distribution to all visitors, create a membership flyer sent out monthly to all members, introduce yoga and meditation classes to be offered at the sanctuary, or create a preschool exploration group led by a skilled bird sanctuary leader filled with stories, short walks, and arts and crafts.

Step 7

Keep a volunteer journal.

Write all your feelings about volunteering with your local bird sanctuary. Did you learn about the birds in your area? Did you have fun with planning an event for its members? Will you continue to volunteer with the bird sanctuary?

Step 8

Make a display board.

Place your display board in a high trafficked area. Post pictures of birds that live at the sanctuary. List the address of the bird sanctuary so that people will know where to find it.

Step 9

Spread awareness.

Tell everyone you know about the bird sanctuary! Ask your friends, family, and neighbors to visit and support the sanctuary.

Step 10

Send thank-you notes.

Remember to thank the staff for showing you the ropes around the bird sanctuary. See Sample 4.

Sample 1—Record Keeping

Bird sanctuary: The Wardel Bird Sanctuary

Spoke with: Doris Williams Date: January 28th
Phone number: 548-0921 Contact time: 11:10 a.m.
E-mail: Doris.Williams@WardelBirdSanctuary.com
Requirements: Volunteer Application needed to be filled out
Regular volunteer positions: Visitor Center, Mailings, Crane Shop and Gardening_____
Fall Fair special event volunteer opportunities (positions): Bell ringer, children's games, home and garden, set up/take down, ticket sales, country store, and beverage tent
Birds and Brunch Event volunteer opportunities (First Sunday of every month): Baked goods needed
When are you available? Weekends only

Sample 2—List of What I Have to Offer

I'm great at gardening
I'm a good baker
Task oriented
Outgoing

Sample 3—Event Planner

Event: Soaring the Sky
Date: Saturday, March 12th   Time: All Day
Music: Theresa Estes, Harpist, will volunteer 2 hours to play at event.
Phone number: 548-8374 Time: 11:00 a.m.–1:00 p.m.
Type of Food: Banana nut bread and assorted muffins
Type of drink: Flavored iced tea
Supplies needed: Napkins and paper cups
Special requests: Tables and chairs will need to be set up that morning.
Guest list:

Guest	Invite Sent	Will Attend	Guest	Invite Sent	Will Attend
Mr. & Mrs. Wade	❏	❏	Serena Vickers	❏	❏
Ms. B. Jamison	❏	❏	Mr. Henry Danes	❏	❏
Chandra Thom	❏	❏	Mrs. G. Marshall	❏	❏
Mrs. R. Hart	❏	❏	Olivia Kemp	❏	❏
Mr. Bill Opal	❏	❏	Mr. W. Aragon	❏	❏
Mr. and Mrs. Fink	❏	❏	Mrs. Julia Dillon	❏	❏

Betty Gables	❑	❑	Chelsea Zuniga	❑	❑
Jenny Monroe	❑	❑	Ellen Gabriel	❑	❑
Carol Bailey	❑	❑	David Sweet	❑	❑
Mrs. M. Brady	❑	❑	Mr. C. Ingleman	❑	❑
Katie Donovan	❑	❑	Mrs. Dotty Garcia	❑	❑
Mr. Lou Green	❑	❑	Prof. F. Jennings	❑	❑
Teeter Pinwinkle	❑	❑	Humphrey Cage	❑	❑
Ms. Ava Roper	❑	❑	Gia Geddings	❑	❑
Hector Garcia	❑	❑	Mrs. D. Stuart	❑	❑
Judd H. King	❑	❑	Claudette Moon	❑	❑
Mr. Pete Hagle	❑	❑	Mr. and Dr. Wynn	❑	❑
Mrs. J. Hollar	❑	❑	Campbell Nixon	❑	❑
Cody Michaels	❑	❑	Laura Votipka	❑	❑
Mrs. Erin Knight	❑	❑	Mr. E. Clarke	❑	❑
Dr. and Mrs. Lee	❑	❑	Arden Peters	❑	❑
Ms. Sandra Cho	❑	❑	Carlos Valdez	❑	❑
Mr. Eddie Barnes	❑	❑	Mrs. C. Traylor	❑	❑
Mrs. L. Graves	❑	❑	Alan Sullivan	❑	❑
Shiloh Shands	❑	❑	Ms. Dolly Serna	❑	❑
Mickey Zuniga	❑	❑	Vivla Hill	❑	❑
Nell Foster	❑	❑	Mr. Patrick Camp	❑	❑
Heather Woods	❑	❑	Julian Davis	❑	❑
Mr. Monte Craig	❑	❑	Beth Russionello	❑	❑

Sample 4—Thank-You Note

To the Staff and Members of the Wardel Bird Sanctuary,
It has been such a pleasure volunteering for this wonderful bird refuge.
I've learned so much about birds and their habitat. I can't wait to share my
experiences with my classmates.

Thank you,

Miguel Rosales

Time spent with cats is never wasted.—Sigmund Freud

Activity 5

Help find Homes for Unwanted Cats and Dogs

Helping to find homes for cats and dogs is a wonderful animal service! It changes animal's lives forever.

Step 1

Make contact.

Call your local animal shelter. Let them know that you would like to help with pet adoption. Find out what the requirements are for volunteering with the animal shelter and if you need to complete any briefings or orientations for volunteering with the animal shelter. See Sample 1.

Step 2

Set up a pet adoption booth.

Decide where you want to set your pet adoption booth. I suggest setting one up at your local pet supply store. You'll get the people traffic you want and plenty of attention and awareness for your local animal shelter because if families aren't ready to add a loving pet to their home just yet, they'll know where to go when they are. Be sure to get permission from the animal shelter and the pet supply store's management. See Sample 2.

Step 3

Be prepared.

Be sure to have all the proper adoption forms available for a forever pet family to fill out. Remember to voice the advantages for pet adoption. You can let people know that shelter adoption fees are usually much less than the cost of an animal purchased at a pet store or breeder. Also, remind them that their new pet is more likely to be already vaccinated, dewormed, and spayed or neutered. See Sample 3.

Step 4

Make an adoption counseling form.

Make a counseling form to hand out to families. This way, they can do a personal assessment to see if they're ready to adopt a pet. Be sure to explain realistic expectations of the time, effort, and money required to sustain a lifelong relationship with their cat or dog. Remember to also add important information such as how to treat your pet, dog training classes, medical services, and behavioral therapy. See Sample 4.

Step 5

Pet profile.

Have a pet profile on hand for every pet you're trying to find a home for. Get the information from the animal shelter. You can depend on responsible shelters to screen the animals for good health and temperament. When animals are relinquished by owners, the shelter staff should make every attempt to collect a thorough history of that pet. Also, as staff and volunteers spend time with the animals, they should try to learn as much as they can about these animals as well as those who come to the shelter as strays. See Sample 5.

Step 6

Take pictures.

Have a digital camera and a photo printer on hand to take pictures of the pet and the new family.

Give them the picture to take home and post on their refrigerator to remember the day they adopted their new loving pet.

Step 7

Make a display board.

Post your display board at school, at a local club, or maybe your local pet supply store. Show pictures of the cats and dogs that are waiting for a forever home. Post the advantages of adopting a pet. Have fun with your display board as you express the importance of adopting unwanted cats and dogs.

Step 8

Keep a journal.

Write down all your experiences with helping to find homes for the cats and dogs at the animal shelter. Did you make any friends? Did you end up adopting a cat or dog?

Step 9

Help spread the word.

Tell everyone you know to tell everyone they know about the cats and dogs at the animal shelter waiting for a wonderful home. These animals are truly in need of a loving family and deserve a good life.

Step 10

Send thank-you notes.

Thank everyone that helped you with your crusade to find homes for cats and dogs. Thank your parents for their support. Thank the animal shelter for their help and assistance. And most important, verbally thank the families that are adopting these loving animals. See Sample 6.

Sample 1—Record Keeping

Animal shelter: South Shore Animal Shelter
Spoke with: Bernard Simpson   Date: March 24th
Phone number: 478-5892 Contact time: 9:30 a.m.
E-mail: Bernard.Simpson@SouthShoreAnimalShelter.com
Volunteer requirements: Fill out volunteer application
Volunteer position: Public Relations/Advertising

Sample 2—Pet Adoption Booth Planning

Location of Booth: PetSmart Pet Supply Store
Contact: Terry McCutcheon
Date: Saturday, May 16 & Sunday, May 17   Time: 9 a.m.–5 p.m.
How many dogs? 6 per day
How many cats? 6 per day
Pet adoption goal: To have 24 pets adopted the entire weekend

Sample 3—Supply List

Adoption paperwork
Receipt book/cash box
Adoption counseling forms
Table
Chairs
Digital camera
Photo printer

Sample 4—Adoption Counseling Form

Adoption Counseling Form

Have you adopted a pet before? Y or N

Do you have a pet now? Y or N

The last time I had a dog I was: 2- 10 yrs oldMore than 10 years ago

Within the last year

My pet needs to be good with:

children   elderly   other cats   other dogs

My pet will primarily be:

an inside dog   an outside dog   an inside cat   an outside cat

My pet needs to be alone for:

4 hours or fewer per day   8-10 hours per day   12 hours per day

When I'm at home I want

my pet to be by my side:

All the time   Some of the time   Little of the time

I will walk my dog:

Everyday   4 times a week   3 times a week   Once a week

When I'm not at home my pet will spend all of its time:

In a crate   In the Garage   in the yard   Loose in the house

Confined to one room

I want a guard dog: Y or N

I want my dog to hunt with me: Y or N

I want my pet to be playful: Y or N

I want my pet to be laid back: Y or N

I am comfortable doing some training with my pet: Y or N

to improve manners such as jumping on others,

pulling on a leash, and stealing food.

I'm ready to teach my children how to be patient and kind to a new pet: Y or N

I am interested in adopting a pet with special needs, medical and behavioral: Y or N

How much do you think it costs for the care of your pet? (food, medical, boarding, toys, etc.)$ _____

Sample 5—Pet Profiles

Dog

Name: Marley

Breed: Labrador Retriever Mix
Size: Med. 20-60 lbs
Color: Brown/Chocolate—With White Markings
Sex: Female
Age: 7 or 8 months
Marley is:
good with kids
good with dogs and cats
up to date with shots
Spayed
I'm an adorable little girl. I was recently rescued from the pound. I'm sweet, lovable and very playful.

Cat

Name: Patches
Breed: Domestic Shorthair
Color: White w/ Black markings
Sex: Male
Age: Young Adult
Patches is:
Neutered
up to date with shots
Not good with other cats or dogs
Patches is a charming young fellow. He plays hard and loves hard. He is very outgoing and is curious about everything. He also loves to be outside.

Dog

Name: Sawyer
Breed: Schnauzer/Terrier Mix
Size: Small 15 lbs
Color: Black
Sex: Male
Age: 2 years
Sawyer is:
good with kids
good with dogs
up to date with shots
Neutered
I'm very cute and very affectionate. I also love to have my belly scratched.

Cat

Name: Stormie
Breed: Domestic Short Hair Calico
Color: Multicolor
Sex: Female
Age: Adult
Stormie is:
Spayed
Up to date with shots
Good with other cats
Not good with dogs
Stormie is very friendly. She loves to cuddle and will follow you everywhere. She is very passive. Stormie has been in a foster care home for five months.

Dog

Name: Rafferty
Breed: Maltese/Poodle Mix
Size: Small 10 lbs
Color: White
Sex: Male
Age: Young Adult—Unknown Age
Rafferty is:
good with kids
good with dogs
up to date with shots
neutered
I'm very playful, fun loving, and extremely outgoing. I love to cuddle too.

Cat

Name: Sweetie Pie
Breed: Domestic Shorthair
Color: Gray, White, and Dark Brown
Sex: Female
Age: Adult
Sweetie Pie is:
spayed
declawed

up to date with shots
Not good with other cats or dogs
Sweetie Pie is a sweetie! She is very shy and is easily spooked by new nois-es. She will crawl on your lap to nestle and will purr loudly. She cannot be outside because she does not have claws to defend herself with. She was found as a stray and never claimed.

Sample 6—Thank-You Note

To the Staff of South Shore Animal Shelter,
Thank you so much for assisting me with the adoption of 24 cats and dogs. I learned so much about the importance of finding homes for these beau-tiful and loving pets. I hope we can do it again soon.
Thanks,

Jonathan Wiley

Dogs laugh, but they laugh with their tails.
—Max Eastman, Enjoyment of Laughter

Activity 6

Help Sponsor a Guide Dog

To help sponsor a guide dog for people with visual impairment or people who are blind, you're potentially making these individuals' lives more independent.

Step 1

Make contact.

Make contact with an organization to express your commitment by wanting to sponsor a dog. Before you call, have some knowledge about what guide dogs do and how important they are to people who are visually impaired. Decide what type of sponsorship you want to do. There are several types of sponsorships. You can sponsor a puppy, a guide dog, a guide dog recipient, or a team (guide dog and the guide dog recipient), a puppy kit, feeding one dog per month, guide dog graduation kit, a leather harness, spaying or neutering one student, feeding one dog during a six-month period, travel expenses for one student, and room and board for one student. Take a look at the program costs and speak to your parents about what would be best for you and your family. www.guidedogsofamerica.org See Sample 1.

Step 2

Plan of action.

How will you raise money for your sponsorship? Make a list of businesses and offices where you plan on placing your donation jar. Be creative with your jar and explain clearly what it's for. See Sample 2.

Step 3

Time frame.

Decide how long you want to on keep your donation jars at your planned locations. Verify with the offices and businesses for approval of your time frame. See Sample 3.

Step 4

Keep track.

Keep track of where you've left your donation jars. Check them regularly. Decide with your parents, what days and times you plan on checking them. Keep a calendar to remind yourself. See Sample 4.

Step 5

Guest speaker.

Locate a person in your area who has a visual impairment or is blind who has a guide dog. Invite that person to be a guest speaker at your school or club you may belong to, with permission of course. Ask that person to show your audience how their guide dog helps him or her on a regular basis. See Sample 5.

Step 6

Make pamphlets.

Now that you have learned all there is to know about guide dogs, make a pamphlet with important information listed inside. Hand them out to the audience.

Step 7

Journal.

Write down all your thoughts about guide dogs. What did you learn? Do you think they're important? Why?

Step 8

Display board.

Post pictures of guide dogs and how they help people who have a visual impairment or who are blind. Make a pocket for your pamphlets so that people can take important information home with them. Who knows, maybe they will be inspired to sponsor a guide dog too!

Step 9

Make others aware.

Spread the awareness of guide dogs.

Step 10

Thank your guest speaker, businesses, and parents.

Remember to write thank-you notes to the people who helped you in your guide dog sponsorship and awareness. See Sample 6.

Sample 1—Record Keeping

Organization: Guide Dogs of America
Spoke with: Jay Bormann   Date: December 27
Phone number: 818-362-5834   Contact time: 2:15 p.m.
E-mail: mail@guidedogsofamerica.org
What type of sponsorship will you try to raise money for: Puppy Sponsorship
      $4,000.00_____

Sample 2—Plan of Action

How will you raise money? I plan on making jars to place at various locations for money donations
How many jars will you make? 37 Goal: To earn $1.00 for each jar a day. That would raise $6,660.00
Locations:

Business: Mom's office
Manager:
How many jars? 1
Jar location: On her desk

Business: Dad's work
Manager: Tina Lopez
How many jars: 1
Jar location: At the front desk

Business: PetSmart
Manager: Douglas Peebles
How many jars? 10
Jar location: 1 for each cashier

Business: Barking Lot Grooming
Manager: Patty Andrews
How many jars: 1
Jar location: Main counter

Business: Arlington Pet Center
Manager: Rita Johnson
How many jars? 1 for each cashier
Jar location: 1 for each cashier

Business: Pet Corner
Manager: Leonard Jordan
How many jars? 2
Jar location: 1 for each cashier

Business: Petco
Manager: William Stojanik
How many jars? 10

Business: Arthur's Grooming
Manager: Melinda Hennley
How many jars? 1

Jar location: 1 for each cashier

Business: Gallery of Pets
Manager: Kimberly Gilliard
How many jars? 1
Jar location: Cashier station

Business: Pampered Pet Center
Manager: Ashley Dobbs
How many jars? 5
Jar location: 1 for each cashier

Jar location: Main counter

Business: Paw Print Grooming
Manager: Victoria Bloom
How many jars? 1
Jar Location: Main counter

Business: The Pet Nanny
Manager: Ricky and Janet Ingles
How many jars? 1
Jar location: Main counter

Sample 3—Time Frame

Business	Time Frame	Approved
Mom's office	January 4—July 4	❏
Dad's work	January 4—July 4	❏
PetSmart	January 4—July 4	❏
Barking Lot Grooming	January 4—July 4	❏
Arlington Pet Center	January 4—July 4	❏
Pet Corner	January 4—July 4	❏
PetCo	January 4—July 4	❏
Arthur's Grooming	January 4—July 4	❏
Gallery of Pets	January 4—July 4	❏
Paw Print Grooming	January 4—July 4	❏
Pampered Pet Center	January 4—July 4	❏
The Pet Nanny	January 4—July 4	❏

Sample 4—Keeping Track

January

Sun	Mon	Tues	Wed	Thurs	Fri	Sat
1	2	3	4 Drop off Jars	5	6	7
8	9	10	11	12	13	14
15	16	17	18	19	20	21 PetSmart PetCo

22	23	24	25	26	27	28
		The Pet Nanny	Arlington Pet Cntr/ Pet Cnr	Arthur's Groom./ Gallery of Pets	Paw Print Groom./ Pamper. Pet Cntr	Barking Lot Groom.

29	30	31
		Mom's Office/Dad's Office

Business	Date	Amount Collected
Mom's office	January 31	$81.20
Dad's work	January 31	$94.47
PetSmart	January 21	$257.57
Barking Lot Grooming	January 28	$31.75
Arlington Pet Center	January 25	$103.05
Pet Corner	January 25	$43.48
PetCo	January 21	$265.85
Arthur's Grooming	January 26	$27.94
Gallery of Pets	January 26	$34.56
Paw Print Grooming	January 27	$18.38
Pampered Pet Center	January 27	$117.63
The Pet Nanny	January 24	$28.00
Total:		$1103.88

Sample 5—Guest Speaker Planner

Guest Speaker: Penelope Finley
Phone number: 476-8374 E-mail: Penelope.Finley@emailaddress.com
Location of event: My House
Date: March 30th Time: 4:30 p.m.
Audience: Girl Scout Troop
Supplies: Food: Chicken/cheese quesadillas, punch, napkins

Sample 6—Thank-You Note

To the Management and Staff of PetSmart,
I would like to thank you for your support to allow me to place a collection jar at every cashier's station to help raise money to sponsor a guide

dog. Your staff and customers donated $677.72 over the six-month peri-
od of the donation collection. I couldn't have met my goal without your
help.

Thank you,

Olive LaRue

If happy little bluebirds fly beyond the rainbow, why oh why can't I?
—E. Y. Harburg, American Lyricist

Activity 7

Build Birdhouses

This is a great project for the whole family.

Step 1

Educate yourself.

Before you begin, you'll have to do a little research about birdhouses. Find out what kinds of birds will use the birdhouses you build, how many you should build for your yard, and where to place them. You'll need to keep in mind how to protect your birdhouses from predators. It may be safer to mount the birdhouses on PVC or metal poles, instead of trees or fences. Trees and fence posts give many predators easy access to the birdhouse. Also, what size of birdhouse do you need? What kind of paint should you use and why? Do you need to add a perch on the front?

Step 2

Birdhouse plan.

After your research, locate a free birdhouse plan or draw and create your own. Remember to include the specifications if you decide to design the birdhouse yourself. See Sample 1.

Step 3

Supply list.

After you've drawn your blueprints of your birdhouse, make a list of the proper tools you'll need to build your project. See Sample 2.

Step 4

Build your birdhouse.

Have fun as you begin to build your birdhouse! Let your parents help you cut the wood with the saw. Always take extra precautions when using a hammer and a saw.

Step 5

Reproduce your birdhouse blueprint.

Make copies of your birdhouse blueprint and the step-by-step directions of how to build your birdhouse. Remember to include the supply list.

Step 6

Nurture your birdhouses.

Help the birds build their nest by placing a bag or basket near the birdhouse with items such as dried grass, moss, short sticks, human or dog hair from a hair brush, and flower petals. Also, face your birdhouses away from the prevailing winds of spring and summer, if possible.

Step 7

Watch the birds.

From a distance and without scaring the birds, watch them enjoy their new home.
What do you think? Do you feel proud?

Step 8

Make a display board.

Post pictures of your birdhouses. Include the type of birds that live in them and why it's important to build houses for wild birds.

Step 9

Keep a journal.

Write about your entire experience from start to finish. Continue to add journal entries about the family of birds that live in the birdhouses.

Step 10

Spread awareness.

You should be very proud of yourself! Share your excitement with others as you express the joys of having built your birdhouses.

Sample 1—Birdhouse Planning

Birdhouse specifications based on research:

Type of Bird: Bluebird
House floor (inches): 5 x 5
House depth (inches): 8
Hole above Floor (inches): 6
Diameter of Hole (inches): 1?
Height above Ground (feet): 5–10
Use 1/4–1/2 inch exterior plywood, cedar, redwood, fir, or pine
Important Notes:
Because bluebirds return to the same birdhouse each season, I cannot move the birdhouse once I've positioned it in the yard.
Bluebirds are very territorial. They require a minimum of 1.5 acres per pair. I cannot place more than one birdhouse in the yard if I don't have enough space.

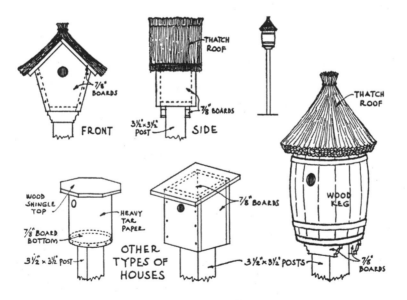

Sample 2—Supply List

Hammer: Make sure you have a sturdy hammer. One with a claw on the backside is helpful if you need to remove any nails.

Screwdriver: A screwdriver is usually needed. There are two main types of screwdrivers: a Phillips head screwdriver (the end has a small cross) or a standard screwdriver (end is straight.) The type needed depends on the type of screw that you will be using. Match the screwdriver to the screw or vice versa. You may also use a screw bit of a power drill or an automatic screwdriver. Both of these allow you to use less force when screwing in the fastener.

Drill and bits: You will need a drill to make the entrance hole for birdhouses. You will also use a drill to predrill holes for nails and screws, making sure the fastener goes in easier as well so it does not split the wood. The part of the drill that actually makes the hole is called a bit. You will need various size bits for making the holes for drainage, ventilation, entrance holes, as well as for predrilling the fastener holes. Wood-boring bits are used for entrance holes for houses. Because entrance hole sizes vary depending on the type of bird who will be using the house, check the birdhouse directions. 1/8 and 1/4 inch bits are great for making the prefastener holes and for drainage and ventilation.

Saw: Circular saws are wonderful for cutting the lengths of wood for bird feeders and birdhouses. You can use a hand saw, but you will use a lot more energy and time to cut the wood. You can also have a lumber yard or home improvement center cut the wood for you.

T-square: T-squares are large rulers used in woodworking. They are used to measure the wood and also will assist you in marking the wood so you get straight cuts or line up the screws straight.

Screws, nails, hinges, fasteners: You can use either screws or nails to keep the birdhouse or feeder together. Nails are a bit easier to use. Make sure nails are galvanized (keeps them from rusting because the house will be outdoors) and made of steel. Finishing nails, ones with small heads, will make your house look better when completed, but ones with larger heads are easier for beginners.

If you decide to use screws, your feeder or house should last longer because the screws will hold the wood more securely as it ages and weathers. Wood screws have a point at the end to help them screw into the wood. Choose screws no longer than about 1? inches long. It is helpful to predrill a hole then screw in the screws. Make sure the drill bit you use is a tiny bit smaller than the screw, so the screw holds the wood tightly. Birdhouses and feeders need a hinge so that the top or side opens. Of course, for feeders, you need to be able to get the seed inside the feeder. Houses need a hinged top or side so that you can clean it out as well as periodically check on the nestlings. A fastener is used to keep the feeder or house closed. There are many types of hinges and fasteners you can use. Some are strictly functional while others are decorative as well as useful. Make sure they have no sharp edges. Take a walk down your hardware store's fastener aisle and choose ones that suit your needs.

Gloves—Gloves are very important to wear as you check on the nestlings. Checking on a nestling should only become necessary to make sure you have a functioning birdhouse or to clean it out when birds are not occupying it. Never ever touch a baby bird with or without your gloves. Birds will abandon their nest and baby birds if they smell your human scent. If you don't have gloves with you, thoroughly rub your hands in dirt. This could also eliminate your human scent.

Our perfect companions never have fewer than four feet.—Colette

Activity 8

Volunteer at a Veterinarian's Office

This activity is great for those who want to care for animals and those who are interested in a career in the veterinary profession.

Step 1

Make contact.

Make a list of several veterinarian offices in your area. Make contact with each one of them and introduce yourself. Ask about their volunteer programs. Express your desire to volunteer at a veterinarian office. Choose one that fits your volunteer needs. See Sample 1.

Step 2

What do you have to offer?

Do you have any special skills? What are you good at doing? Are you outgoing? Make a list of all your attributions and experience. See Sample 2.

Step 3

Be committed.

Remember, once you begin your volunteer work with the veterinarian's office the staff and animals are counting on you to be there. Sit down with your parents and make a realistic volunteer schedule. Write the days and times in your monthly calendar.

Step 4

Learn about pet safety.

Did you know that you can take a class through the American Red Cross that offers a pet first aid book? Learn how to care for an animal if there's an emergency situation. This will help you with your experience while you're volunteering at the veterinarian office.

Step 5

Help schedule appointments.

Become an active volunteer. Help the staff schedule the appointments. Learn what questions you'll need to ask each pet parent. Have a cheat sheet handy when you are scheduling the appointments.

Step 6

Be innovative.

Think of something that the veterinarian's office doesn't already have. Here are some ideas: comfort pets after recovery, write condolence cards to families who have lost a pet, and start up a veterinarian runners program that can deliver and pick up animals to and from the veterinarian's office.

Step 7

Make a display board.

Share your experiences by making a display board with pictures from the veterinarian's office. Have fun and be creative!

Step 8

Keep a volunteer journal.

Write all your thoughts about your volunteer work at the veterinarian's office.

Step 9

Help spread the word.

Tell everyone about your local veterinarian's office. Let them know that it's very important to have their pet's health screened on a regular basis.

Step 10

Thank the staff.

Give the staff a thank-you note for teaching you various jobs at the office. See Sample 3.

Sample 1—Record Keeping

Veterinarian office: Pet Vet Animal Clinic
Spoke with: Garth Crawford, DVM   Date: September 8th
Phone number: 547-8503 Contact time: 9:50 a.m.

Volunteer position available: Filing and Record Keeping
Schedule: Mon., Wed., & Fri. 3—5 p.m.

Sample 2—List of my Skills and Talents

Have great attention to detail
Outgoing
Great at task managing
Good note taker
Works great with others
Great with animals

Sample 3—Thank-You Note

To Dr. Crawford and Staff,
Thank you for allowing me the opportunity to work in such a great learning environment. I learned so much about the care you give to all your pet patients. You truly are heroes. I can't wait to tell all my friends about my volunteer experience.
Thank you again,

Joseph Martin

The greatness of a nation and its moral progress can be judged
by the way its animals are treated.—Mohandas Gandhi

Activity 9

Volunteer at a Zoo

If you love wild animals, volunteering at your local zoo is a fantastic way to be an animal hero. Not only do zoos provide a great opportunity to learn about exotic animals in a safe environment, they also are wonderful places to make friends. Most zoos offer a wide variety of volunteer programs to choose from, all of which are great ways to help wild animals.

Step 1

Find your nearest zoo.

Introduce yourself and let the volunteer coordinator know why you want to volunteer. Find out what their qualifications are, and if there are any age limitations for different kinds of volunteer work. There's always something for everyone! See Sample 1.

Step 2

What do you have to offer?

Are you outgoing? Are you ready to learn something new? Make a list of all your skills and talents. See Sample 2.

Step 3

Be committed.

It's most likely that a zoo will initially have mandatory training that each volunteer will have to attend. Once you've completed your training, be committed to your volunteer schedule. Usually at zoos, they have specific time commitment schedules already set for summer volunteer opportunities. Find out what they are and speak to your family about it. See Sample 3.

Step 4

Plan a field trip.

Coordinate a field trip for your classmates or circle of friends. Organize the field trip with your principal or parents of friends. Request the proper transportation to and from the zoo. See Sample 4.

Step 5

Plan for a show.

Every zoo usually has a wonderful exhibit. Find out what their exhibits are and arrange for one for your field trip.

Step 6

Coloring activity.

Ask your classmates to draw a picture of their experience at the zoo. Ask them to write one or two sentences of what they liked about the zoo. Collect all the drawings and give them to the zoo to show them just how much everyone loves the zoo.

Step 7

Keep a volunteer journal.

Write your thoughts and express your feelings about your volunteer work at the zoo.

Step 8

Make a display board.

Be creative! Include fun facts about your local zoo. Post pictures of your experiences and new friends.

Step 9

Spread awareness.

Encourage others to visit and to become a member of the zoo. There are many benefits of being a member of the zoo. They also have programs designed to fit everyone's needs and budget.

Step 10

Be thankful.

Thank the staff and fellow volunteers for the experience you've shared with them. See Sample 5.

Sample 1—Record Keeping

Zoo: City Park Zoo
Spoke with: Volunteer Office   Date: April 18th
Phone number: 441-3247 Contact time: 1:35 p.m.
E-mail: volunteers@cityzoo.com
Qualifications: Applicants who are under 16 years of age must have an adult chaperone
Application period: June 1—August 1 / for the following summer volunteer program
Training course: Begins late September
10 consecutive Saturdays from 9 a.m.—4 p.m.
Special requests: Annual tuberculosis test required of all volunteers

Sample 2—List of my Skills and Talents

Detail oriented
A good time keeper
Creative
Action oriented
Good note taker
Great team player

Sample 3—Volunteer Schedule

November

Sun	Mon	Tues	Wed	Thurs	Fri	Sat
1	2	3	4	5	6	7 Training 9-4
8	9	10	11	12	13	14 Training 9-4
15	16	17	18	19	20	21 Training 9-4
22	23	24	25	26	27	28 Training 9-4
29	30					

Following Summer

June

Sun	Mon	Tues	Wed	Thurs	Fri	Sat
1	2	3	4	5	6	7
						Volunteer 9-4
8	9	10	11	12	13	14
						Volunteer 9-4
15	16	17	18	19	20	21
						Volunteer 9-4
22	23	24	25	26	27	28
			Family Vacation	Family Vacation	Family Vacation	Family Vacation
29	30					

Sample 4—Field Trip Planner

Principal: Dr. Ben Lockhart
Date of Field Trip: October 25   Time of Field Trip: 9 a.m.—2 p.m.
Grade Level: 7th grade
Transportation: School bus provided by school district
Permission Forms Required: Yes
Number of Students: 127
Number of Teachers: 4   Number of Chaperones Required: 9
Zoo Contact Person: Sally Barnaby, Events Coordinator, 441-3267
Special Events: Bird Show will be conducted for class at 9:30 a.m.

Sample 5—Thank-You Note

Training Staff and Volunteer Coordinators,
I would like to take this opportunity to thank you for this most wonderful experience. I have learned so much about the care and safety of the zoo animals. I have made so many friends, all who share the same love and passion for these beautiful animals as I do. Thank you for all your help and support.
Your friend,
Alexis Phillips, Volunteer

Ocean: A body of water occupying two-thirds of a world made
for man—who has no gills.—Ambrose Bierce

Activity 10

Volunteer at an Aquarium

Promote the Importance of your Local Aquarium
The opportunities for volunteering at an aquarium are educational and
hands-on learning.

Step 1

Make contact.

Find out if your local aquarium has a youth volunteer program. Fill out the
necessary applications for your volunteerism. Be prepared to answer questions like, "Why do you want to be a youth volunteer at the aquarium?"
"What should the aquarium expect from you?" See Sample 1.

Step 2

What do you have to offer?

After you find out about your local aquarium's volunteer program, make a
list of your best qualities. There is always something at an aquarium that
you can help with, whether it's promoting new memberships, preparing
food for the animals, painting fish on children's cheeks, wearing a penguin
costume, volunteering at the gift shop, or giving tours of the aquarium.
See Sample 2.

Step 3

Be committed.

It's important that you commit yourself to your volunteer work. Talk to
your parents about how many hours you can commit each week or month.

Step 4

Plan a field trip.

Coordinate a field trip for your school. Organize in advance with your
principal to request the proper transportation and paperwork for your

field trip. See Sample 3.

Step 5

Plan for a lecturer.

Many aquariums have marine biologists who can explain about ocean ecology and marine animals. Schedule a lecture on the day that your school has its field trip. See Sample 4.

Step 6

Hand out expert cards.

Make cards for all your classmates. Pass them out after your aquarium's learning session. See Sample 5.

Step 7

Keep a journal.

Write down all your experiences. What is your favorite exhibit? Are you afraid of the sharks? Have you learned a lot about sea creatures? Express your feelings about your volunteerism with the aquarium.

Step 8

Make a display board.

Share all your experiences by making a display board with pictures of your new friends, animals and employees.

Step 9

Spread the word.

Tell everyone you know how amazing the Aquarium is! Tell them about the sting rays, turtles, fish, and dolphins. Everyone should enjoy what your aquarium has to offer.

Step 10

Send thank-you notes.

Write a thank-you note to the volunteer coordinator and the staff at the aquarium. Thank them for all their help and guidance. Also, don't forget to thank your parents who supported you through your volunteer work at the aquarium. See Sample 6.

Sample 1—Record Keeper

Name of Aquarium: The Bay Aquarium

Spoke with: Dee Dee Barker   Date: October 1st

Phone number: 785-5803 Contact time: 1:20 p.m.

Address: 7539 Coral Reef

Volunteer Program Requirements: Must be 16 years old, 2 shifts per month with a one-year commitment, attend a volunteer orientation, and three-week training course 1 night a week for three weeks.

Volunteer Positions Available:

Guest Services Volunteer—Greeting and assisting guests with any general questions about the aquarium's exhibits and show schedules.

Show Assistant Volunteer—Help with penguin show with set-up and breakdown and crowd control.

Husbandry Volunteer—Preparing animal's food, cleaning animal areas, watering plants, and assisting with general duties.

Sample 2—List of my Skills and Talents

Very outgoing

Good with animals

Great organization skills

I love biology

Very creative

Sample 3—Field Trip Planner

Name of Aquarium: The Bay Aquarium

Spoke with: Holly Jackson Date: January 10th

Phone number: 785-5803 Contact time: 10:30 a.m.

Principal's name: Dr. J. J. Goldblum

Junior high school's name: Kimbrough Junior High School

Will there be bus transportation to and from school? Yes

Date of field trip: March 8th   Time of Field Trip: 9:00 a.m.–2:00 p.m.

Grade level: 8

How many students will be attending? 66

How many teachers will be attending? 3

How many chaperones will be attending? 9

Special events: Students will listen to lecture: The JASON Project: Monster

Storms Auditorium Project
Notes: Students will need to bring their own lunch or bring money to eat
at the aquarium's cafe

Sample 4—Planner for Lecturer
Name of speaker: Dr. Ben Spangle
Time of lecture: 11:00 a.m.–12:30 p.m.

Sample 5—Expert Cards

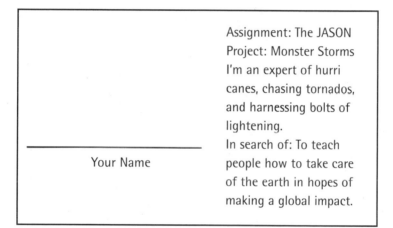

Assignment: The JASON
Project: Monster Storms
I'm an expert of hurri
canes, chasing tornados,
and harnessing bolts of
lightening.
In search of: To teach
people how to take care
of the earth in hopes of
making a global impact.

Your Name

Sample 6—Thank-You Note
To the staff of Bay Aquarium,
Thank you for all your support and teachings. I've never worked with so
many enthusiastic people. I really appreciate all the fun we had.
Your friend,

Avery Charles, Volunteer

Appendix A

Log Hours—Tracking Sheet

Date	Name of Volunteer Director	Signature of Volunteer	Volunteer Activity	Time in	Time Out	Total Time
				___AM ___PM	___AM ___PM	___HRS ___MIN.
				___AM ___PM	___AM ___PM	___HRS ___MIN.
				___AM ___PM	___AM ___PM	___HRS ___MIN.
				___AM ___PM	___AM ___PM	___HRS ___MIN.
				___AM ___PM	___AM ___PM	___HRS ___MIN.
				___AM ___PM	___AM ___PM	___HRS ___MIN.
				___AM ___PM	___AM ___PM	___HRS ___MIN.
				___AM ___PM	___AM ___PM	___HRS ___MIN.

Appendix B

Certificate of Completion

You're an Ultimate Volunteer

Super Job!

This Certifies That

_____
Your Name Here

Has Completed the Following Service Act with Great Enthusiasm and Hard Work

_____
Volunteer Activity

_____
Date

_____
Volunteer Director

Glossary

advertise. To make a public announcement of, with careful deliberation.

animal husbandry. The care of domestic and wild animals.

auction. A public sale in which property or items of merchandise are sold.

collage. An artistic composition of materials and objects pasted over a surface.

compost. Decomposed remnants of organic materials.

donation drive. A gift to a fund or cause, typically for charitable reasons. A donation may take various forms, including cash, services, clothing, toys, food, accommodation, blood, or new or used items.

ecological awareness. The study of the detrimental effects of human civilization on the environment, and being aware of these effects.

fund-raiser. A social function held for raising money for a specific charity or nonprofit organization.

greenhouse. A Structure built of glass or plastic, in which humidity can be controlled for nurturing or protection of plants.

guide dog. A dog trained to guide a person who is blind or a person with a visual impairment.

humanitarian awareness. Someone who is devoted to the promotion of human welfare and being responsive to the need. It is based on a view that all human beings deserve respect and dignity and should be treated as such.

nonprofit organization. An organization whose primary objective is to support an issue or matter of private interest or public concern for noncommercial purposes, without concern for monetary profit. A nonprofit organization may be involved in a wide range of areas relating to the arts, social issues, charities, early childhood education, health care, politics, religion, research, sports, or some other endeavor.

nursery. A place where plants are grown.

organic. Organic materials derive from living organisms. It is essentially all living things on Earth.

promote. To make others aware. To make something popular.

recycle. The reprocessing of used materials into new products.

refuge. Protection for species from hunting, predation, or competition.

rescue. Operations that usually involve the saving of life, or prevention of injury.

sanctuary. A place where animals live and are protected.

scavenger hunt. A game in which individuals or teams seek to find a number of specific items, or perform tasks, as given in a list. The goal is either to complete the list first, or to achieve the highest score within a given time limit.

sponsor. One who assumes responsibility for another person or a group.

volunteer. A person who performs a service for his or her community.

Acknowledgments

I would like to acknowledge the many important people who have made this book a reality.

Special thanks to Bruce H. Franklin of Westholme Publishing. You have made this process more than enjoyable. I want to thank you for seeing the need for a book like this. With your help, I now have the ability to reach and inspire so many families and children. For that, I am grateful.

I would also like to thank the wonderful people at Volunteermatch.org. To Greg Baldwin for taking the time to express the need for volunteerism at a young age through the book's foreword. Thanks to Jason Willett and Julia Lee for believing in this project and supporting the book in so many vital areas.

To Trudi Gershenov for creating a fantastic book cover. The cover is timeless and was just what I was hoping for!

Thanks to Denise McIntyre for going through my book page-by-page and giving wonderful feedback and for making my manuscript the best that it could be.

For my Web site designer Val Laolagi. Thank you for taking my vision and making www.UltimateVolunteer.com come alive. You are an incredible artist.

To my good friend, Junel Jeffrey. Thank you for supporting me through this journey. Your friendship and motivating words will never be forgotten.

Sincere gratitude to Jaelyn Coates for providing me with added support in compiling a list of non-profit organizations for my Web site. Your hard work is appreciated.

To Thomas Maxwell and musical artist Scott Keeton. Thank you for providing the music for my Web site. The sound was just was I was looking for.

To my parents, Maria and Isidro Garza. Thank you for giving me unconditional love. I couldn't ask for better role models. Your shining examples have made me a better person.

To my In-laws, Richard and Deanna Maxwell. Thank you for loving me as your daughter. You are a positive and encouraging force that I have learned to depend on. I truly feel like I gained two extra parents when I married Marc.

To my sister-in-law, Kristi. You are my rock that I can't imagine being without. I love you so much and thank God everyday for having you in my life.

To my girlfriends, Alegra, Jill, and Cyndee. Thank you for your friendship, love and support. I love you all like sisters.

And finally to my entire family, which includes: the Family Garza, the Family Maxwell, the Family Droege, the Family Campa, the Family Salazar, the Family Thompson, the Family Morado, the Family Villarreal, the Family Rutkowski, the Family Greenamoyer, the Family Goode, the Family Johnson, the Family Charrette, and the Family Soliz. Thank you for giving me so much love and support. As a family you bring such joy to my life and have given me so many wonderful memories. You have no idea what it means to me to have all of you in my life. I am so proud to have you as my family. I love you all very much.